# Harvard Business Review

on

# COLLABORATING EFFECTIVELY

# The Harvard Business Review
## Paperback series

If you need the best practices and ideas for the business challenges you face—but don't have time to find them—*Harvard Business Review* **paperbacks** are for you. Each book is a collection of HBR's inspiring and useful perspectives on a given management topic, all in one place.

### The titles include:

Harvard Business Review on Advancing Your Career

Harvard Business Review on Aligning Technology with Strategy

Harvard Business Review on Building Better Teams

Harvard Business Review on Collaborating Effectively

Harvard Business Review on Communicating Effectively

Harvard Business Review on Finding & Keeping the Best People

Harvard Business Review on Fixing Health Care from Inside & Out

Harvard Business Review on Greening Your Business Profitably

Harvard Business Review on Increasing Customer Loyalty

Harvard Business Review on Inspiring & Executing Innovation

Harvard Business Review on Making Smart Decisions

Harvard Business Review on Managing Supply Chains

Harvard Business Review on Rebuilding Your Business Model

Harvard Business Review on Reinventing Your Marketing

Harvard Business Review on Succeeding as an Entrepreneur

Harvard Business Review on Thriving in Emerging Markets

Harvard Business Review on Winning Negotiations

# Harvard Business Review

## on

# COLLABORATING EFFECTIVELY

**Harvard Business Review Press**

Boston, Massachusetts

Library of Congress Cataloging-in-Publication Data

Harvard business review on collaborating effectively.
    p. cm. — (The Harvard business review paperback series)
    ISBN 978-1-4221-6264-4 (alk. paper)
    1. Organizational effectiveness.   2. Management.   3. Teams in the workplace.   I. Harvard business review.
    HD58.9.H377 2011
    658.4'022—dc22

                                                2011006054

# Contents

# When Internal Collaboration Is Bad for Your Company

*by Morten T. Hansen*

**INTERNAL COLLABORATION IS ALMOST** universally viewed as good for an organization. Leaders routinely challenge employees to tear down silos, transcend boundaries, and work together in cross-unit teams. And although such initiatives often meet with resistance because they place an extra burden on individuals, the potential benefits of collaboration are significant: innovative cross-unit product development, increased sales through cross-selling, the transfer of best practices that reduce costs.

But the conventional wisdom rests on the false assumption that the more employees collaborate, the better off the company will be. In fact, collaboration can just as easily undermine performance. I've seen it happen many times during my 15 years of research in this area.

In one instance, Martine Haas, of Wharton, and I studied more than 100 experienced sales teams at a large information technology consulting firm. Facing fierce competition from such rivals as IBM and Accenture for contracts that might be worth $50 million or more, teams putting together sales proposals would often seek advice from other teams with expertise in, say, a technology being implemented by the prospective client. Our research yielded a surprising conclusion about this seemingly sensible practice: The greater the collaboration (measured by hours of help a team received), the worse the result (measured by success in winning contracts). We ultimately determined that experienced teams typically didn't learn as much from their peers as they thought they did. And whatever marginal knowledge they did gain was often outweighed by the time taken away from their work on the proposal.

The problem here wasn't collaboration per se; our statistical analysis found that novice teams at the firm actually benefited from exchanging ideas with their peers. Rather, the problem was determining when it makes sense and, crucially, when it doesn't. Too often a business leader asks, How can we get people to collaborate more? That's the wrong question. It should be, Will collaboration on this project create or destroy value? In fact, to collaborate well is to know when not to do it.

This article offers a simple calculus for differentiating between "good" and "bad" collaboration using the concept of a collaboration premium. My aim is to ensure that groups in your organization are encouraged to

## Idea in Brief

Are you promoting cross-unit collaboration for collaboration's sake? If so, you may be putting your company at risk. Collaboration can deliver tremendous benefits (innovative offerings, new sales). But it can also backfire if its costs (including delays stemming from turf battles) prove larger than you expected.

To distinguish good collaboration from bad, estimate three factors:

- **Return:** "What cash flow would this collaboration generate if executed effectively?"

- **Opportunity cost:** "What cash flow would we pass up by investing in this project instead of a non-collaborative one?"

- **Collaboration costs:** "What cash flow would we lose owing to problems associated with cross-unit work?"

Would the return exceed the combined opportunity and collaboration costs? If yes, put that collaborative project in motion.

work together only when doing so will produce better results than if they worked independently.

## How Collaboration Can Go Wrong

In 1996 the British government warned that so-called mad cow disease could be transferred to humans through the consumption of beef. The ensuing panic and disastrous impact on the worldwide beef industry over the next few years drove food companies of all kinds to think about their own vulnerability to unforeseen risks.

The Norwegian risk-management services firm Det Norske Veritas, or DNV, seemed well positioned to take advantage of the business opportunity this represented by helping food companies improve food safety.

## Idea in Practice

In deciding whether to launch a collaborative effort, managers can fall victim to three common errors. By understanding these errors, you stand a better chance of avoiding them.

**Overestimating the Return**

Many companies place a mistakenly high economic value on collaboration. Often, the expected results don't materialize.

> **Example:** Daimler's $36 billion acquisition of Chrysler in 1998 failed to deliver the promised synergies between the two automakers. In 2007, Daimler sold 80% of Chrysler for a mere $1 billion.

**Ignoring Opportunity Costs**

Executives often fail to consider opportunities they would forgo by devoting resources to a particular collaborative project. They don't evaluate *non*-collaborative activities that might have higher potential.

> **Example:** Risk-management services firm DNV decided to combine the expertise, resources, and customer bases of two business units—standards certification and risk-management consulting. The goal? To cross-sell services to help food companies improve food safety. DNV estimated the collaboration's return as $40 million.

But DNV never compared the food-industry opportunity that required cross-unit collaboration with other industry opportunities that wouldn't require collaboration. One opportunity in IT could have been pursued

Founded in 1864 to verify the safety of ships, DNV had expanded over the years to provide an array of risk-management services through some 300 offices in 100 countries.

In the fall of 2002 DNV began to develop a service that would combine the expertise, resources, and customer bases of two of the firm's business units: standards certification and risk-management consulting.

by the consulting unit alone, and it had more potential than the food opportunity. But because many of the consulting unit's experts were tied up with the food initiative, progress on the IT opportunity was constrained. The cost of the forgone opportunity was $25 million in revenue.

## Underestimating Collaboration Costs

In most companies, it's difficult to get people in different units to work together effectively because:

- People don't want to share resources or customers.

- They resent taking on extra work if it provides little recognition and no financial incentive.

- They have conflicting priorities; for example, some people are dedicated to the initiative full-time, while others aren't.

These tensions create problems that, combined with opportunity costs, can eat into the collaboration's potential—and produce a collaboration *penalty.*

*Example:* At DNV, competition over customers between the two units caused tensions that ultimately scotched 50% of cross-selling engagements. That amounted to $20 million in collaboration costs. Added to the $25 million opportunity cost for the noncollaborative IT opportunity, total costs were $45 million—$5 million *over* the collaborative food opportunity's expected return of $40 million.

The certification business had recently created a practice that inspected large food company production chains. The consulting business had also targeted the food industry as a growth area, with the aim of helping companies reduce risks in their supply chains and production processes.

Initial projections for a joint effort were promising: If the two businesses collaborated, cross-marketing their services to customers, they could realize 200% growth from 2004 to 2008, as opposed to 50% if they operated separately. The net cash flow projected for 2004 through 2008 from the joint effort was $40 million. (This and other DNV financial figures are altered here for reasons of confidentiality.)

The initiative was launched in 2003 and run by a cross-unit team charged with cross-selling the two types of services and developing new client relationships with food companies. But the team had trouble capitalizing on what looked like a golden opportunity. Individual business unit revenue from areas where the existing businesses had been strong—Norway for consulting services, for example, and Italy for certification—continued to grow, exceeding projections in 2004. But the two units did little cross-pollination in those markets. Furthermore, the team couldn't get much traction in the United Kingdom and other targeted markets, which was particularly disappointing given that the certification group had established good relations with UK food regulators in the years following the outbreak of mad cow disease.

As new business failed to materialize, the consulting group, which was under pressure from headquarters to improve its overall results in the near term, began shifting its focus from the food industry to other sectors it had earlier targeted for growth, weakening the joint effort. The certification group continued to make the food industry a priority, but with the two groups' combined food industry revenue lagging behind projections in 2005, DNV abandoned the initiative it had launched with such optimism only two years before.

## Knowing When (and When Not) to Collaborate

DNV's experience is hardly atypical. All too often plans involving collaboration among different parts of an organization are unveiled with fanfare only to collapse or fizzle out later. The best way to avoid such an outcome is to determine *before* you launch an initiative whether it is likely to yield a *collaboration premium.*

A collaboration premium is the difference between the projected financial return on a project and two often overlooked factors—opportunity cost and collaboration costs. In simple form:

$$\frac{\textit{Projected return} - \textit{Opportunity cost} - \textit{Collaboration costs}}{\textit{Collaboration premium}}$$

The projected return on a project is the cash flow it is expected to generate. The opportunity cost is the cash flow an organization passes up by devoting time, effort, and resources to the collaboration project instead of to something else—particularly something that doesn't require collaboration. Collaboration costs are those arising from the challenges involved in working across organizational boundaries—across business units, functional groups, sales offices, country subsidiaries, manufacturing sites. Cross-company collaboration typically means traveling more, coordinating work, and haggling over objectives and the sharing of information. The resulting tension that can develop between parties often creates significant costs: delays in getting to market, budget

7

overruns, lower quality, limited cost savings, lost sales, damaged customer relationships.

Including collaboration costs makes this analysis different from the usual go/no-go decision making for proposed projects. Obviously, such costs can't be precisely quantified, especially before a project is under way. Still, with some work you can arrive at good approximations. Given how much time managers already spend estimating the return on a project—and, occasionally, the associated opportunity cost—it makes sense to take the additional step of estimating collaboration costs, particularly because they can doom a project.

If, after going through this exercise, you don't foresee a collaboration premium—or if a collaboration *penalty* is likely—the project shouldn't be approved. Indeed, this sort of analysis might have helped DNV steer clear of a promising but ultimately costly business venture.

## Avoiding Collaboration That Destroys Value

In calculating the collaboration premium, it's important to avoid several common errors.

### Don't Overestimate the Financial Return

Whether because of enthusiasm for collaboration or the natural optimism of managers, many companies place a mistakenly high value on collaboration. Especially when a team's work appears to be a model of collaboration— the parties freely share resources and cooperate in resolving differences while coming up with nifty ideas—it may be easy to overlook the fact that the work is actually generating little value for the company. Never forget that the goal of collaboration is not collaboration but, rather, business results that would be impossible without it.

In numerous well-known instances, collaboration premiums failed to materialize. Daimler's $36 billion acquisition of Chrysler in 1998—with its promise of synergies between the two automakers—and the sale nine years later of 80% of Chrysler for a pitiful $1 billion constitute only the most conspicuous recent example. But collaboration's benefits are usually overvalued in much more mundane settings. Recall how the experienced sales teams at the IT consulting firm that Martine Haas and I studied shared expertise as a matter of course during the preparation of project proposals—never stopping to seriously consider whether they in fact benefited from doing so.

### Don't Ignore Opportunity Costs

Executives evaluating any proposed business project should take into account the opportunities they will forgo by devoting resources to that project. If the project requires collaboration, it's important to consider alternative noncollaborative activities with potentially higher returns. The opportunity cost is the estimated cash flow from the most attractive project *not* undertaken.

DNV didn't overestimate the potential financial return of its food initiative, but it did fail to assess the opportunity cost. "There was no consensus at the top level that food was interesting or a priority," said one senior manager. "We had not evaluated the food opportunity against other industry segments." In fact, food was only

## Collaboration During a Recession

**INTERNAL COLLABORATION, OFTEN INTENDED** to spur new product development or increase revenue, may seem a low priority in a period of profit-focused cost cutting. That's a big mistake. Collaboration ought to be a crucial element of your recession strategy, because it will allow you to generate profits by exploiting existing assets—to do more with what you already have.

Wells Fargo headed into the 2002 recession with an enviable record of cross-selling 3.8 products, on average, per household customer. In 2002 the bank increased this number to an astonishing 4.2—that is, it sold nearly one additional financial product for every two customers in the middle of a recession, squeezing additional profits out of its existing customer base.

Three kinds of collaboration are especially valuable in a recession:

### Cross-Selling

Follow the example of Wells Fargo and start programs to sell additional products to existing customers, who are more likely than those who don't know you to buy from you. This can increase your sales and lower the cost of selling, thus raising your profit per customer.

### Best-Practice Transfer

Identify units in your company that are particularly efficient at certain activities—for example, the sales office with the lowest personnel costs—and get other units to follow their example. This can improve productivity and lower costs per employee.

### Cross-Unit Product Innovation

Find ways of combining existing technologies, products, and brands to create new products, and brands to create new products and services. This is cheaper than developing them from scratch and more likely to succeed because you draw on tested intellectual property. It can increase the number of new products, speed them to market, and lower development costs.

one of several sectors—including information technology, health care, and government—that DNV's consulting unit had targeted in 2001 as offering growth potential for its risk-management services. The opportunity in IT, which the consulting unit could have pursued on its own, undoubtedly had more potential. The unit made progress in 2004 generating new business in this sector, but it was constrained by a shortage of qualified consultants, some of whom were tied up with the food initiative. To pursue the food initiative, the consulting unit had to forgo additional business from the IT opportunity. I estimate the cost of this forgone opportunity at $25 million or more in lost cash flow.

**Don't Underestimate Collaboration Costs**
In most companies it's difficult to get people in different units to work together effectively. Issues relating to turf, such as the sharing of resources and customers, often make groups resistant to collaboration. Individuals may resent taking on extra work if they don't get additional recognition or financial incentives. Even when collaboration delivers obvious and immediate benefits to those involved (for example, one unit's software package solves another's current problem), blending the work of two units that usually operate independently creates impediments.

These costs, which should be assessed before committing to a cross-unit project, can be tough to identify and quantify. And they will vary depending on the collaboration culture of an organization. But although they can be reduced over time through companywide efforts to foster collaboration, it's a mistake to underestimate them in the hope that collaboration can be mandated or will naturally improve during the course of a project.

As DNV decided whether to move forward with its food initiative, the project managers failed to consider the substantial collaboration costs the company would incur because it wasn't set up to collaborate. Mistrust between the consulting and certification units escalated as they tried—unsuccessfully, and with much quarreling—to build a common customer database. "All the team members tried to protect their own customers," one manager in the certification group admitted. Because of the reluctance to share customer relationships, the team had to significantly reduce its estimates of the revenue to be generated by cross-selling.

Individual members of the cross-unit team were also pulled by conflicting goals and incentives. Only one team member was dedicated to the initiative full-time; most people had to meet individual targets within their respective units while also working on the joint project. Some people got a dressing down from their managers if their cross-unit work didn't maximize their own unit's revenue.

Even those who saw the benefits of the initiative found it hard to balance their two roles. "We all had personal agendas," said one senior manager in the certification group. "It was difficult to prioritize the food initiative and to pull people out of their daily work to do the cross-area work."

Although assigning a financial number to collaboration costs is difficult, I estimate that the cash flow sacrificed as a result of tension between the two groups, which scotched probably one in two cross-selling opportunities, was roughly $20 million.

Had the likely opportunity and collaboration costs of DNV's food-safety project been estimated, the project would have looked decidedly less attractive. In fact, managers would have seen that, rather than a collaboration premium, it was likely to yield a collaboration penalty of something like $5 million—that is, the projected return of $40 million less an opportunity cost of $25 million and collaboration costs of $20 million.

## How Collaboration Can Go Right

That's not the end of DNV's story, however. Several months after the firm abandoned the food-safety initiative, Henrik Madsen was named CEO. He had seen firsthand the poor business results, wasted management effort, and ill will spawned by the initiative, having been head of the certification unit at the time. But he also believed that performance could be enhanced by collaboration at the traditionally decentralized DNV.

Madsen quickly reorganized the firm into four market-oriented business units and began looking for collaboration opportunities. His executive committee systematically evaluated all the possible pairings of units and identified a number of promising opportunities for cross-selling. The unit-by-unit analysis also revealed something else important: pairings that offered no real opportunities for collaboration—an insight that would prevent wasted efforts in the future.

The disciplined process prompted the committee to assess the potential financial return of each opportunity. Estimates totaled roughly 10% of the company's revenue at the time. The projected returns helped the committee prioritize options and assess the opportunity cost of choosing one over another. On the basis of these findings, along with an assessment of likely collaboration costs, the company launched a round of collaboration initiatives.

One of these involved the maritime unit, which provides detailed classification of vessels for companies in the shipping industry, and the IT unit, which specializes in risk-management services for IT systems in many industries. Because ships today operate using sophisticated computer systems, someone needs to help shipping companies manage the risk that those systems will malfunction at sea. There was a clear opportunity to sell IT's services to the maritime unit's customers—if effective collaboration could be achieved between the two units. That opportunity has already borne fruit: The IT unit won a contract to develop information systems for a huge cruise ship being built by a longtime customer of the maritime unit.

The IT unit has also collaborated with the company's energy business to jointly sell services to oil and drilling companies—another opportunity identified in the executive committee's review. That effort enhances the IT unit's service offering with the energy unit's oil and gas industry expertise, a package that most IT competitors can't match. The two units split the revenue, which creates incentives for both.

In pursuing opportunities like these, DNV has worked to reduce some of the typical costs of collaboration. Annie Combelles, the chief operating officer of the IT business, says there was an obvious market for her unit's services among customers of the maritime and energy units. "My concern was that those units understand what we could deliver," she says. "My concern was internal, not external." The IT group appointed a business development manager who had worked at DNV for 12 years, including a stint in the maritime unit, and had a broad personal network within the company. This made him a trusted and knowledgeable liaison to the maritime and other units, reducing potential conflict between them and the IT unit.

What's more, the IT unit has moved cautiously in trying to capitalize on opportunities for internal collaboration. Although the maritime group's longtime relationship with the cruise ship operator provided entrée for the information technology group, maritime didn't want any missteps from IT to jeopardize that valuable relationship. IT therefore initially proposed a risk-assessment project in nonvital areas of the ship such as the "hotel" function, which included the Wi-Fi network, gambling computers, and the 5,000 personal computers to be used by guests. It evaluated each of these systems and identified 30 risks. This success led to a project involving vital areas of the ship, such as the power-management and positioning systems.

DNV's renewed effort to encourage cross-unit collaboration is a work in progress that has nonetheless already produced some hard results: The portion of the IT unit's sales that came from cross-unit collaboration climbed from almost nothing to 5% in 2008, and is projected to be 10% in 2009 and 30% the following year.

---

Business leaders who trumpet the benefits of working together for the good of the organization are right in seeing collaboration's tremendous potential. But they should temper those exhortations with the kind of analysis I've described here, which provides needed discipline in deciding when collaboration creates—or destroys—value. Ideally, as organizations become better at collaboration, through incentives and shifts in corporate culture, the associated costs will fall and the percentage of projects likely to benefit will rise.

Although the collaboration imperative is a hallmark of today's business environment, the challenge is not to cultivate more collaboration. Rather, it's to cultivate the right collaboration, so that we can achieve the great things not possible when we work alone.

**MORTEN T. HANSEN** is a professor at the University of California at Berkeley. He is the author of *Collaboration: How Leaders Avoid the Traps, Create Unity, and Reap Big Results* (Harvard Business Review Press, 2009).

Originally published in April 2009. Reprint R0904G

# Which Kind of Collaboration Is Right for You?

*by Gary P. Pisano and Roberto Verganti*

IN AN ERA WHEN great ideas can sprout from any corner of the world and IT has dramatically reduced the cost of accessing them, it's now conventional wisdom that virtually no company should innovate on its own. The good news is that potential partners and ways to collaborate with them have both expanded enormously in number. The bad news is that greater choice has made the perennial management challenge of selecting the best options much more difficult. Should you open up and share your intellectual property with the community? Should you nurture collaborative relationships with a few carefully selected partners? Should you harness the "wisdom of crowds"? The fervor around open models of collaboration such as crowdsourcing notwithstanding, there is no best approach to leveraging the power of outsiders. Different modes of collaboration involve different strategic trade-offs. Companies that choose the wrong mode risk falling behind in the relentless race to develop new technologies, designs, products, and services.

All too often firms jump into relationships without considering their structure and organizing principles—what we call the *collaborative architecture*. To help senior managers make better decisions about the kinds of collaboration their companies adopt, we have developed a relatively simple framework. The product of our 20 years of research and consulting in this area, it focuses on two basic questions: Given your strategy, how open or closed should your firm's network of collaborators be? And who should decide which problems the network will tackle and which solutions will be adopted?

Collaboration networks differ significantly in the degree to which membership is open to anyone who wants to join. In totally open collaboration, or crowdsourcing, everyone (suppliers, customers, designers, research institutions, inventors, students, hobbyists, and even competitors) can participate. A sponsor makes a problem public and then essentially seeks support from an unlimited number of problem solvers, who may contribute if *they* believe they have capabilities and assets to offer. Open-source software projects such as Linux, Apache, and Mozilla are examples of these networks. Closed networks, in contrast, are like private clubs. Here, you tackle the problem with one or more parties that *you* select because you deem them to have capabilities and assets crucial to the sought-after innovation.

Collaboration networks also differ fundamentally in their form of governance. In some the power to decide

# Idea in Brief

As potential innovation partners and ways to collaborate with them proliferate, it's tough deciding how best to leverage outsiders' power.

To select the right type of collaboration options for your business, Pisano and Verganti recommend understanding the four basic collaboration modes. These modes differ along two dimensions: *openness* (can anyone participate, or just select players?) and *hierarchy* (who makes key decisions—one "kingpin" participant or all players?).

- In the *open, hierarchical* mode, anyone can offer ideas but your company defines the problem and chooses the solution.

- In the *open, flat* mode, anyone can solicit and offer ideas, and no single participant has the authority to decide what is or isn't a valid innovation.

- In the *closed, hierarchical* mode, your company selects certain participants and decides which ideas get developed.

- In the *closed, flat* mode, a select group is invited to offer ideas. But participants share information and intellectual property and make critical decisions together.

Each mode has trade-offs. For example, open networks (whether hierarchical or flat) produce many ideas, but screening them is costly. What to do? Choose modes best suited to your capabilities. For instance, if you can evaluate ideas cheaply but no single participant has all the necessary expertise to shape the innovation, use an open, flat collaboration.

which problems are most important, how they'll be solved, what constitutes an acceptable solution, and which solutions should be implemented is completely vested in one firm in the network: the "kingpin." Such networks are hierarchical. Other networks are flat: The players are equal partners in the process and share the power to decide key issues.

# Idea in Practice

## Understanding Your Collaboration Options

| Dimension | Advantages | Challenges | When to use |
|---|---|---|---|
| Open | • You attract a wide range of possible ideas from domains beyond your experience. | • Screening all the ideas is time-consuming and expensive.<br><br>• The best idea generators prefer closed networks, where their ideas are more likely implemented. | • You can evaluate proposed solutions cheaply.<br><br>• You don't know what users want. |
| Closed | • You receive the best solution from a select knowledge domain. | • You have to know how to identify the right knowledge domain and pick the right parties. | • You need a small number of problem solvers.<br><br>• You know the correct knowledge domain and parties to draw on. |
| Hierarchical | • Kingpins control the direction and value of the innovation. | • The right direction may be unclear. | • You have the capabilities and knowledge needed to define the problem and evaluate proposed solutions. |
| Flat | • Players share the costs, risks, and technical challenges of innovating. | • All parties must arrive at mutually beneficial solutions. | • No single player in the network has the necessary breadth of perspective or capabilities to solve the innovation problem. |

## Examples of Collaboration Options

| Mode | Example |
| --- | --- |
| Open, hierarchical | Through InnoCentive.com, sponsor companies post scientific problems that are smaller pieces of their larger R&D program. Anyone can offer solution ideas. The "kingpins" understand the relevant technologies and user needs and can coordinate collaborators' work. |
| Open, flat | In open-source software community Linux, anyone can participate, define valid innovations, and use any code they deem useful. |
| Closed, hierarchical | Home-products design company Alessi draws on the talents of 200 independent designers. It decides who participates in its network, which concepts get developed, and which products are launched. |
| Closed, flat | IBM invited a few select partners to join its Microelectronics Joint Development Alliance for developing semiconductor technologies such as memory and chip-manufacturing processes. Each member has a voice in how technologies are developed. |

## Choosing Your Collaboration Approach

Select the collaboration mode that best suits your capabilities and strategy.

**Example:** In developing the iPhone and its applications, Apple initially used closed, hierarchical networks, where it could better control components influencing users' experiences. But once the iPhone was established, Apple defined a growth strategy hinging on adding software functionality and applications. Because it knew it couldn't anticipate all the applications iPhone users might value, it switched to an open, flat network: It introduced a kit allowing third-party developers to create applications based on the iPhone OS platform and to provide them to users directly through the device.

Discussions of collaborative innovation in both academic journals and the popular media often wrongly link "openness" only with "flatness"—and even suggest that open, flat approaches are always superior. The notion is deeply flawed, however.

As the exhibit "The four ways to collaborate" shows, there are four basic modes of collaboration: a closed and hierarchical network (an *elite circle*), an open and hierarchical network (an *innovation mall*), an open and flat network (an *innovation community*), and a closed and flat network (a *consortium*).

When figuring out which mode is most appropriate for a given innovation initiative, a firm should consider the trade-offs of each, weighing the modes' advantages against the associated challenges and assessing the organizational capabilities, structure, and assets required to manage those challenges. (See the exhibit "How to choose the best mode of collaboration.") Its executives should then choose the mode that best suits the firm's strategy.

## Open or Closed Network?

The costs of searching for, screening, and selecting contributors grow as the network becomes larger and can become prohibitive. So understanding when you need a small or a large number of problem solvers is crucial. Closed modes, obviously, tend to be much smaller than open ones.

When you use a closed mode, you are making two implicit bets: that you have identified the knowledge

## The four ways to collaborate

*There are two basic issues that executives should consider when deciding how to collaborate on a given innovation project: Should membership in a network be open or closed? And, should the network's governance structure for selecting problems and solutions be flat or hierarchical? This framework reveals four basic modes of collaboration.*

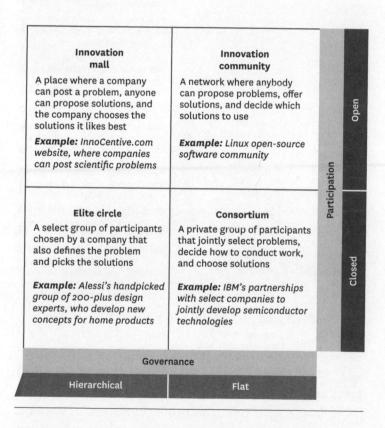

| | |
|---|---|
| **Innovation mall** | **Innovation community** |
| A place where a company can post a problem, anyone can propose solutions, and the company chooses the solutions it likes best | A network where anybody can propose problems, offer solutions, and decide which solutions to use |
| *Example: InnoCentive.com website, where companies can post scientific problems* | *Example: Linux open-source software community* |
| **Elite circle** | **Consortium** |
| A select group of participants chosen by a company that also defines the problem and picks the solutions | A private group of participants that jointly select problems, decide how to conduct work, and choose solutions |
| *Example: Alessi's handpicked group of 200-plus design experts, who develop new concepts for home products* | *Example: IBM's partnerships with select companies to jointly develop semiconductor technologies* |

Participation: Open / Closed

Governance: Hierarchical / Flat

domain from which the best solution to your problem will come, and that you can pick the right collaborators in that field. Alessi, an Italian company famous for the

# How to choose the best mode of collaboration

*When selecting a mode of collaborative innovation, executives need to consider the distinct strategic trade-offs of each mode. Below are some important advantages and challenges of the different approaches to collaboration, and examples of capabilities, assets, processes, and kinds of problems that make each easier to carry out.*

**Advantage:** You receive a large number of solutions from domains that might be beyond your realm of experience or knowledge, and usually get a broader range of interesting ideas.

**Challenge:** Attracting several ideas from a variety of domains and screening them.

**Enablers:** The capability to test and screen solutions at low cost; information platforms that allow parties to contribute easily; small problems that can be solved with simple design tools, or large problems that can be broken into discrete parts that contributors can work on autonomously.

|  |  | Participation | |
|---|---|---|---|
| **Innovation mall** | **Innovation community** | | Open |
| **Elite circle** | **Consortium** | | Closed |
| Governance | | | |
| Hierarchical | Flat | | |

**Advantage:** You control the direction of innovation and who captures the value from it.

**Challenge:** Choosing the right direction.

**Enablers:** The capability to understand user needs; the capability to design systems so that work can be divided among outsiders and then integrated.

**Advantage:** You share the burden of innovation.

**Challenge:** Getting contributors to converge on a solution that will be profitable to you.

**Enablers:** Processes and rules that drive parties to work in concert to achieve common goals.

**Advantage:** You receive solutions from the best experts in a selected knowledge domain.

**Challenge:** Identifying the right knowledge domain and the right parties.

**Enablers:** The capability to find unspotted talent in relevant networks; the capability to develop privileged relationships with the best parties.

postmodern design of its home products, bet that postmodern architecture would be a fruitful domain for generating interesting product ideas and that it could find the best people in that field to work with. It invited 200-plus collaborators from that domain to propose product designs. If you don't know where to look for solutions or who the key players are (and have no way to find out), a closed mode like Alessi's elite circle is a dangerous shot in the dark.

The big advantage of an open network is its potential to attract an extremely large number of problem solvers and, consequently, a vast number of ideas. You do *not* need to identify either the best knowledge domains or the most appropriate experts in those domains. It's like throwing an open house party: You just make it known you are having a party and provide the right inducements, and (you hope) the right people will show up.

With open participation, you don't need to know your contributors. Indeed, the fact that you *don't* know them can be particularly valuable; interesting innovative solutions can come from people or organizations you might never have imagined had something to contribute. That is the concept behind Threadless.com, a largely online retailer of T-shirts, whose designs come from the masses. By operating an innovation mall where 600,000 members submit proposals for about 800 new designs weekly, Threadless gets a steady flow of unusual and singular ideas. (Mall members and visitors to the website vote on the designs, but the Threadless staff makes the final decision on which ones to produce and rewards their creators.)

Open modes, however, have their disadvantages. Notably, they're not as effective as closed approaches in identifying and attracting the best players. That's because as the number of participants increases, the likelihood that a participant's solution will be selected (especially for an ambiguous problem) decreases. The best parties, therefore, prefer to participate in closed relationships. Open modes work best when the spread between the ideal solution and the average solution is not big and the consequences of missing out on a much better solution from an elite player are small.

Open modes are effective only under certain conditions. First, it must be possible to evaluate proposed solutions at a low cost. Sometimes the screening process is extremely cheap and fast. (For instance, it might be easy to assess whether a particular module of software code works or has bugs.) In other cases, though, the only way to find out whether an idea is worth pursuing is through expensive and time-consuming experiments, and you'll want to consider fewer (but better) ideas. The only way to do that is to invite contributions from the problem solvers that you think will have the best chance of providing good ideas. That is, to opt for a closed mode.

Consider the following simple but scary example. You have a serious illness, and you want to find the best possible treatment. Employing an open mode, you post your problem on the internet, ask for advice, and get 50 ideas that look interesting. But immediately, you face two issues. The first is what statisticians refer to as a sample selection problem: Are these the best 50 ideas out there? Maybe the most knowledgeable doctors are so busy treating patients that they don't participate in these forums, and only the doctors who have time on their hands (a bad sign for sure!) responded. The second issue is that you have to invest a lot of time and resources to evaluate the 50 ideas (visiting doctors and so on). Even worse, you may have only one shot at getting the right treatment. (Are you really going to "try out" more than one surgery?) That is why when confronted with a medical problem, we might do some research to identify elite specialists, pick one, and then seek a second opinion from one or two others.

Alessi is in a similar boat. Given the large population of designers, it could easily launch an open design competition for, say, a corkscrew on its website. With its high standing in the world of design, the firm would probably attract many proposals. However, it is not posing technical problems that have one or a few optimal solutions that can be clearly defined, thereby allowing contributors to screen many of their ideas themselves. Alessi is looking for concepts whose value is based on intangible properties such as aesthetics and emotional and symbolic content. Since there is no clear right or wrong answer, Alessi could receive thousands of proposals, creating a massive evaluation burden for the company. And because the company's strategy is to offer products with radical designs that anticipate market needs, its offerings often initially confuse consumers. Therefore it can't shift the evaluation burden to customers by asking them which designs they prefer, as Threadless does. That's why Alessi has to ensure that it will receive a few good ideas from a relative handful of contributors.

Another requirement of open modes is that participating in them must be easy. This is possible when a problem can be partitioned into small, well-defined chunks that players can work on autonomously at a fairly low cost. Someone creating a potential decoration for a Threadless T-shirt doesn't need sophisticated design infrastructure or knowledge of how the company will knit yarns or tailor shirts. The inherently modular structure of the Linux open-source community allows software developers to create code for new features without touching other parts of the application, which has more than four million lines of code. Over the past decade, such open collaboration has been made easier by information platforms that allow participants to make contributions, share work, and observe the solutions of others.

Of course, not all problems can be partitioned into small, discrete chunks. For example, the development of radically new product concepts or product architectures is an integral task that has to be embraced in its entirety. In such cases, closed modes that provide an environment where collaborators can closely interact must be employed. This is what led IBM to invite a handful of selected partners (including Siemens, Samsung, Freescale, Infineon, and STMicroelectronics) to join its Microelectronics Joint Development Alliance consortia for developing semiconductor technologies such as memory, silicon-on-insulator components, and chip-manufacturing processes.

## Flat or Hierarchical Governance?

As discussed earlier, the chief distinction between a hierarchical and a flat form of governance is who gets to define the problem and choose the solution. In the hierarchical form, a specific organization has this authority, which provides it with the advantage of being able to control the direction of the innovation efforts and capture more of the innovation's value. In the flat form, these decisions are either decentralized or made jointly by some or all collaborators; the advantage here is the ability to share with others the costs, risks, and technical challenges of innovating.

Hierarchical governance is desirable when your organization has the capabilities and knowledge needed to define the problem and evaluate proposed solutions. Consider companies that post scientific problems on the innovation mall InnoCentive.com. The problems are generally smaller pieces of the sponsors' much larger R&D programs. These kingpins have a clear understanding of the relevant technologies and markets (user needs and functional requirements) and can define the system configuration and coordinate the work of various collaborators.

Conversely, flat modes work well when no single organization has the necessary breadth of perspective or capabilities. Look again at open-source software projects. These often develop very specific modules of code to address problems that users have encountered (a bug in an existing piece of code or the need for a specific hardware driver). In this case, the users are best positioned to devise and test solutions because they're closest to the problem. Indeed, they usually have discovered the problem in the first place. Or take IBM's microelectronics consortia. Since semiconductor companies other than IBM possessed critical knowledge, skills, and assets needed for microprocessor design, a hierarchical structure would have made no sense.

Flat modes are also appropriate when collaborators all have a vested interest in how a particular problem is solved and will participate only if they get some say in the decisions. For example, all the members of the IBM consortia formed over the years have expected to use in their own factories and product lines the technologies they develop collaboratively. For this reason, IBM and its partners chose a governance structure that provided each a strong voice in how the technology is developed.

Designing incentives—both financial and nonfinancial—that attract external collaborators is crucial with any of the four modes of collaboration. Nonfinancial rewards like high visibility in the job market, an enhanced reputation among a peer group, the psychological fulfillment of pursuing a strong interest, and the chance to use solutions in one's own business can replace or complement monetary rewards. There are no hard rules about which incentives work best with particular forms of collaboration. Although people often associate psychological fulfillment with innovation communities, it can be a powerful incentive in the other modes as well. For example, Alessi not only shares royalties from sales with the designers in its elite circle but also includes their names in product marketing and offers them a high degree of freedom in the design process.

## A Matter of Strategy

Choosing a collaboration mode involves more than understanding the trade-offs. A firm must take into account its strategy for building and capturing value. And as the strategy evolves, the right mode of collaboration might change, too.

Consider the approach that Apple used in developing software for the iPhone and how it changed over time. A key part of Apple's business strategy (across all its products) has been to maintain the integrity of its systems. Indeed, one of the joys (and thus differentiators) of an Apple product is that everything—the machine's hardware, software, and peripherals—seems to work together so seamlessly. Historically, this kept Apple more oriented toward closed modes, where it could better control the components that influenced the user's experience. The company took that approach in developing the first generations of the iPhone as well and relied on elite circles to develop early applications for it.

However, once the iPhone was established, Apple faced the challenge of adding software functionality and applications that would fuel more growth. Our framework helps map out the various options Apple had. It could define the applications it thought would be useful (for example, a way to synchronize the iPhone with various mobile banking systems) and then engage the best software designers to develop them (the elite circle mode again). It could partition the development of particular applications into simple chunks and then go to a bazaar like TopCoder.com and tap hordes of software developers to write code for each chunk (the innovation mall mode). It could release a development package to third-party developers and let them define and create applications that would be useful (the innovation community mode). Or Apple could work jointly with a firm like Intuit to create mobile banking software (the consortium mode). Each of these modes could certainly generate new applications, but each would have a very different impact on the iPhone platform.

To stick with the elite circle mode, Apple needed to feel confident that it knew which applications customers would want and could identify the best partners for creating them. Given the huge variety of potential applications, Apple realized that there was no way that, either alone or with a small group of collaborators, it could anticipate all the applications that an iPhone owner might find useful or just fun. So it opted to encourage a thousand flowers to bloom and allow the market to decide which ones should be picked. This reasoning ruled out the elite circle, the consortium, and the innovation mall. Accordingly, Apple introduced a kit in March 2008 that allows a community of third-party developers to create applications based on the iPhone OS platform and provide them to users directly through the iPhone. (If an application is not free, the developers keep 70% of its revenues and Apple gets 30%.)

The rollout of mobile phones using Android, Google's operating system, could prompt Apple to adopt a two-part collaboration strategy. Since Android is open-source software, it may attract an even larger community of developers than the iPhone. So Apple might decide to supplement the applications developed by third parties with proprietary hardware features conceived by its own staff and created with the help of elite circles of hardware manufacturers. That illustrates another important point: Companies can use a combination of collaboration modes simultaneously to support their strategies.

IBM's successful use of *both* an innovation community and consortia to support the strategy of its server and mainframe computer businesses is an excellent real example. IBM's strategy is to compete on the basis of hardware differentiation and service. Toward that end, the company has striven to commoditize operating systems by embracing Linux and participating actively in the open-source community—one of the first major computer makers to do so. But to continue to differentiate its hardware, IBM needs to stay on the leading edge of microprocessor technology. Given the increasing scale required to keep up with the likes of Intel, IBM turned to its consortia of semiconductor companies, which have shared development costs. This combination of innovation approaches has allowed IBM to gain market share in an intensely competitive and dynamic market.

As IBM illustrates, a key component of strategy is exploiting a firm's unique assets and capabilities. In choosing one or more collaborative modes, a firm's senior managers therefore must ask: Which of our unique assets and capabilities are we trying to enhance the value of? And what's the best way to enhance it?

A firm's collaboration capability itself can be exploited for profit. InnoCentive.com, for example, is a spin-off of an innovation mall developed by Eli Lilly for internal purposes. Alessi is now leveraging the value of its connections with more than 200 designers by assisting companies in other businesses with product design. Alessi helps them identify the designers (usually from its own network) who can best address their specific needs. In return, Alessi receives royalties from sales of the resulting products—which now account for almost 30% of its revenues.

## A New Source of Advantage

As with any strategic variable, collaborative approaches to innovation offer an array of choices and complex trade-offs. As the examples in this article suggest, each approach can be highly effective under the right conditions. Senior managers need to be wary of the notion that one type of collaboration is superior to others. Open is not always better than closed, and flat is not always better than hierarchical.

Developing an effective approach to collaboration starts with a solid understanding of your company's strategy. What is the business problem you want innovation to solve? Are you (like Alessi) trying to create a distinctive product that breaks boundaries? Are you (like IBM) trying to keep up with larger rivals (like Intel and Taiwan Semiconductor) in an intense technology race? Or are you (like Apple today) looking to broadly expand the applications of your product?

Companies must also ask what unique capabilities they bring to the collaborative process. Firms with deep relationships in a space, for example, are much better positioned to exploit an elite circle mode than a newcomer is.

It's not surprising, then, that differences in strategy and capabilities can lead to different kinds of collaboration networks competing against one another in the same industry. Thus, the task of senior leadership in innovation has broadened and become truly strategic. It is no longer just a matter of hiring the most talented and creative people or establishing the right internal environment for innovation. The new leaders in innovation will be those who can understand how to design collaboration networks and how to tap their potential.

**GARY P. PISANO** is the Harry E. Figgie, Jr., Professor of Business Administration at Harvard Business School. **ROBERTO VERGANTI** is a professor of innovation management at the Politecnico di Milano, Italy, and the author of *Design-Driven Innovation* (Harvard Business Review Press, 2009).

**Originally published in December 2008.** Reprint R0812F

# Eight Ways to Build Collaborative Teams

*by Lynda Gratton and Tamara J. Erickson*

**WHEN TACKLING A MAJOR** initiative like an acquisition or an overhaul of IT systems, companies rely on large, diverse teams of highly educated specialists to get the job done. These teams often are convened quickly to meet an urgent need and work together virtually, collaborating online and sometimes over long distances.

Appointing such a team is frequently the only way to assemble the knowledge and breadth required to pull off many of the complex tasks businesses face today. When the BBC covers the World Cup or the Olympics, for instance, it gathers a large team of researchers, writers, producers, cameramen, and technicians, many of whom have not met before the project. These specialists work together under the high pressure of a "no retake" environment, with just one chance to record the action. Similarly, when the central IT team at Marriott sets out to develop sophisticated systems to enhance guest experiences, it has to collaborate closely with independent hotel owners, customer-experience experts, global brand managers, and regional heads, each with his or her own agenda and needs.

Our recent research into team behavior at 15 multinational companies, however, reveals an interesting paradox: Although teams that are large, virtual, diverse, and composed of highly educated specialists are increasingly crucial with challenging projects, those same four characteristics make it hard for teams to get anything done. To put it another way, the qualities required for success are the same qualities that undermine success. Members of complex teams are less likely—*absent other influences*—to share knowledge freely, to learn from one another, to shift workloads flexibly to break up unexpected bottlenecks, to help one another complete jobs and meet deadlines, and to share resources—in other words, to collaborate. They are less likely to say that they "sink or swim" together, want one another to succeed, or view their goals as compatible.

Consider the issue of size. Teams have grown considerably over the past ten years. New technologies help companies extend participation on a project to an ever greater number of people, allowing firms to tap into a wide body of knowledge and expertise. A decade or so ago, the common view was that true teams rarely had more than 20 members. Today, according to our research, many complex tasks involve teams of 100 or more. However, as the size of a team increases beyond

## Idea in Brief

To execute major initiatives in your organization—integrating a newly acquired firm, overhauling an IT system—you need **complex** teams. Such teams' defining characteristics—large, virtual, diverse, and specialized—are crucial for handling daunting projects. Yet these very characteristics can also destroy team members' ability to work together, say Gratton and Erickson. For instance, as team size grows, collaboration diminishes.

To maximize your complex teams' effectiveness, construct a basis for collaboration in your company. Eight practices

hinging on relationship building and cultural change can help. For example, create a strong sense of community by sponsoring events and activities that bring people together and help them get to know one another. And use informal mentoring and coaching to encourage employees to view interaction with leaders and colleagues as valuable.

When executives, HR professionals, and team leaders all pitch in to apply these practices, complex teams hit the ground running—the day they're formed.

20 members, the tendency to collaborate naturally decreases, we have found. Under the right conditions, large teams can achieve high levels of cooperation, but creating those conditions requires thoughtful, and sometimes significant, investments in the capacity for collaboration across the organization.

Working together virtually has a similar impact on teams. The majority of those we studied had members spread among multiple locations—in several cases, in as many as 13 sites around the globe. But as teams became more virtual, we saw, cooperation also declined, unless the company had taken measures to establish a collaborative culture.

## Idea in Practice

The authors recommend these practices for encouraging collaboration in complex teams.

**What Executives Can Do**

- Invest in building and maintaining social relationships throughout your organization.

  *Example:* Royal Bank of Scotland's CEO commissioned new headquarters built around an indoor atrium and featuring a "Main Street" with shops, picnic spaces, and a leisure club. The design encourages employees to rub shoulders daily, which fuels collaboration in RBS's complex teams.

- Model collaborative behavior.

  *Example:* At Standard Chartered Bank, top executives frequently fill in for one another, whether

leading regional celebrations, representing SCB at key external events, or initiating internal dialogues with employees. They make their collaborative behavior visible through extensive travel and photos of leaders from varied sites working together.

- Use coaching to reinforce a collaborative culture.

  *Example:* At Nokia, each new hire's manager lists everyone in the organization the newcomer should meet, suggests topics he or she should discuss with each person on the list, and explains why establishing each of these relationships is important.

**What HR Can Do**

- Train employees in the specific skills required for collaboration: appreciating others, engaging in

As for diversity, the challenging tasks facing businesses today almost always require the input and expertise of people with disparate views and backgrounds to create cross-fertilization that sparks insight and innovation. But diversity also creates problems. Our research shows that team members collaborate more easily and naturally if they perceive themselves as purposeful conversation, productively and creatively resolving conflicts, and managing programs.

- Support a sense of community by sponsoring events and activities such as networking groups, cooking weekends, or tennis coaching. Spontaneous, unannounced activities can further foster community spirit.

*Example:* Marriott has recognized the anniversary of the company's first hotel opening by rolling back the cafeteria to the 1950s and sponsoring a team twist dance contest.

**What Team Leaders Can Do**

- Ensure that at least 20%–40% of a new team's members already know one another.

*Example:* When Nokia needs to transfer skills across business functions or units, it moves entire small teams intact instead of reshuffling individual people into new positions.

- Change your leadership style as your team develops. At early stages in the project, be task-oriented: articulate the team's goal and accountabilities. As inevitable conflicts start emerging, switch to relationship building.

- Assign distinct roles so team members can do their work independently. They'll spend less time negotiating responsibilities or protecting turf. But leave the *path* to achieving the team's goal somewhat ambiguous. Lacking well-defined tasks, members are more likely to invest time and energy collaborating.

being alike. The differences that inhibit collaboration include not only nationality but also age, educational level, and even tenure. Greater diversity also often means that team members are working with people that they know only superficially or have never met before—colleagues drawn from other divisions of the company, perhaps, or even from outside it. We have found that the higher the proportion of strangers on the team and the greater the diversity of background and experience, the less likely the team members are to share knowledge or exhibit other collaborative behaviors.

In the same way, the higher the educational level of the team members is, the more challenging collaboration appears to be for them. We found that the greater the proportion of experts a team had, the more likely it was to disintegrate into nonproductive conflict or stalemate.

So how can executives strengthen an organization's ability to perform complex collaborative tasks—to maximize the effectiveness of large, diverse teams, while minimizing the disadvantages posed by their structure and composition?

To answer that question we looked carefully at 55 large teams and identified those that demonstrated high levels of collaborative behavior despite their complexity. Put differently, they succeeded both because of and despite their composition. Using a range of statistical analyses, we considered how more than 100 factors, such as the design of the task and the company culture, might contribute to collaboration, manifested, for example, in a willingness to share knowledge and workloads. Out of the 100-plus factors, we were able to isolate eight practices that correlated with success—that is, that appeared to help teams overcome substantially the difficulties that were posed by size, long-distance communication, diversity, and specialization. We then interviewed the teams that were very strong in these practices, to find out how they did it. In this article we'll walk through the practices. They fall into four general categories—executive support, HR practices, the strength of the team leader, and the structure of the team itself.

## Executive Support

At the most basic level, a team's success or failure at collaborating reflects the philosophy of top executives in the organization. Teams do well when executives invest in supporting social relationships, demonstrate collaborative behavior themselves, and create what we call a "gift culture"—one in which employees experience interactions with leaders and colleagues as something valuable and generously offered, a gift.

### Investing in Signature Relationship Practices

When we looked at complex collaborative teams that were performing in a productive and innovative manner, we found that in every case the company's top executives had invested significantly in building and maintaining social relationships throughout the organization. However, the way they did that varied widely. The most collaborative companies had what we call "signature" practices—practices that were memorable, difficult for others to replicate, and particularly well suited to their own business environment.

For example, when Royal Bank of Scotland's CEO, Fred Goodwin, invested £350 million to open a new headquarters building outside Edinburgh in 2005, one of his goals was to foster productive collaboration among employees. Built around an indoor atrium, the

## The Research

**OUR WORK IS BASED ON A MAJOR RESEARCH** initiative conducted jointly by the Concours Institute (a member of BSG Alliance) and the Cooperative Research Project of London Business School, with funding from the Advanced Institute for Management and 15 corporate sponsors. The initiative was created as a way to explore the practicalities of collaborative work in contemporary organizations.

We sent surveys to 2,420 people, including members of 55 teams. A total of 1,543 people replied, a response rate of 64%. Separate surveys were administered to group members, to group leaders, to the executives who evaluated teams, and to HR leaders at the companies involved. The tasks performed by the teams included new-product development, process reengineering, and identifying new solutions to business problems. The companies involved included four telecommunication companies, seven financial services or consulting firms, two media companies, a hospitality firm, and one oil company. The size of the teams ranged from four to 183 people, with an average of 44.

Our objective was to study the levers that executives could pull to improve team performance and innovation in collaborative tasks. We examined scores of possible factors, including the following:

**The general culture of the company.** We designed a wide range of survey questions to measure the extent to which the firm had a cooperative culture and to uncover employees' attitudes toward knowledge sharing.

**Human resources practices and processes.** We studied the way staffing took place and the process by which people were promoted. We examined the extent and type of training, how reward systems were configured, and the extent to which mentoring and coaching took place.

**Socialization and network-building practices.** We looked at how often people within the team participated in informal socialization, and the type of interaction that was most common. We also asked numerous questions about the extent to which team members were active in informal communities.

**The design of the task.** We asked team members and team leaders about the task itself. Our interest here was in how they perceived the purpose of the task, how complex it was, the extent to which the task required members of the team to be interdependent, and the extent to which the task required them to engage in boundary-spanning activities with people outside the team.

**The leadership of the team.** We studied the perceptions team members had of their leaders' style and how the leaders described their own style. In particular, we were interested in the extent to which the leaders practiced relationship-oriented and task-oriented skills and set cooperative or competitive goals.

**The behavior of the senior executives.** We asked team members and team leaders about their perceptions of the senior executives of their business unit. We focused in particular on whether team members described them as cooperative or competitive.

In total we considered more than 100 factors. Using a range of statistical analyses, we were able to identify eight that correlated with the successful performance of teams handling complex collaborative tasks.

new structure allows more than 3,000 people from the firm to rub shoulders daily.

The headquarters is designed to improve communication, increase the exchange of ideas, and create a sense of community among employees. Many of the offices have an open layout and look over the atrium—a vast transparent space. The campus is set up like a small town, with retail shops, restaurants, jogging tracks and cycling trails, spaces for picnics and barbecues—even a leisure club complete with swimming pool, gym, dance studios, tennis courts, and football pitches. The idea is that with a private "Main Street" running through the headquarters, employees will remain on the campus throughout the day—and be out of their offices mingling with colleagues for at least a portion of it.

To ensure that non-headquarters staff members feel they are a part of the action, Goodwin also commissioned an adjoining business school, where employees from other locations meet and learn. The visitors are encouraged to spend time on the headquarters campus and at forums designed to give employees opportunities to build relationships.

Indeed, the RBS teams we studied had very strong social relationships, a solid basis for collaborative activity that allowed them to accomplish tasks quickly. Take the Group Business Improvement (GBI) teams, which work on 30-, 60-, or 90-day projects ranging from back-office fixes to IT updates and are made up of people from across RBS's many businesses, including insurance, retail banking, and private banking in Europe and the United States. When RBS bought NatWest and migrated the new acquisition's technology platform to RBS's, the speed and success of the GBI teams confounded many market analysts.

BP has made another sort of signature investment. Because its employees are located all over the world, with relatively few at headquarters, the company aims to build social networks by moving employees across functions, businesses, and countries as part of their career development. When BP integrates an acquisition (it has grown by buying numerous smaller oil companies), the leadership development committee deliberately rotates employees from the acquired firm through positions across the corporation. Though the easier and cheaper call would be to leave the executives in their own units—where, after all, they know the business— BP instead trains them to take on new roles. As a consequence any senior team today is likely to be made up of people from multiple heritages. Changing roles frequently—it would not be uncommon for a senior leader at BP to have worked in four businesses and three geographic locations over the past decade—forces executives to become very good at meeting new people and building relationships with them.

### Modeling Collaborative Behavior

In companies with many thousands of employees, relatively few have the opportunity to observe the behavior of the senior team on a day-to-day basis. Nonetheless, we found that the perceived behavior of senior executives plays a significant role in determining how cooperative teams are prepared to be.

## Collaboration Conundrums

**THESE ARE FOUR TRAITS** that are crucial to teams—but also undermine them.

### Large Size

Whereas a decade ago, teams rarely had more than 20 members, our findings show that their size has increased significantly, no doubt because of new technologies. Large teams are often formed to ensure the involvement of a wide stakeholder group, the coordination of a diverse set of activities, and the harnessing of multiple skills. As a consequence, many inevitably involve 100 people or more. However, our research shows that as the size of the team increases beyond 20 members, the level of natural cooperation among members of the team decreases.

### Virtual Participation

Today most complex collaborative teams have members who are working at a distance from one another. Again, the logic is that the assigned tasks require the insights and knowledge of people from many locations. Team members may be working in offices in the

---

Executives at Standard Chartered Bank are exceptionally good role models when it comes to cooperation, a strength that many attribute to the firm's global trading heritage. The Chartered Bank received its remit from Queen Victoria in 1853. The bank's traditional business was in cotton from Bombay (now Mumbai), indigo and tea from Calcutta, rice from Burma, sugar from Java, tobacco from Sumatra, hemp from Manila, and silk from Yokohama. The Standard Bank was founded in the Cape Province of South Africa in 1863 and was prominent in financing the development of the diamond fields and later gold mines. Standard Chartered was formed in 1969 through a merger of the two

same city or strung across the world. Only 40% of the teams in our sample had members all in one place. Our research shows that as teams become more virtual, collaboration declines.

### Diversity

Often the challenging tasks facing today's businesses require the rapid assembly of people from multiple backgrounds and perspectives, many of whom have rarely, if ever, met. Their diverse knowledge and views can spark insight and innovation. However, our research shows that the higher the proportion of people who don't know anyone else on the team and the greater the diversity, the less likely the team members are to share knowledge.

### High Education Levels

Complex collaborative teams often generate huge value by drawing on a variety of deeply specialized skills and knowledge to devise new solutions. Again, however, our research shows that the greater the proportion of highly educated specialists on a team, the more likely the team is to disintegrate into unproductive conflicts.

banks, and today the firm has 57 operating groups in 57 countries, with no home market.

It's widely accepted at Standard Chartered that members of the general management committee will frequently serve as substitutes for one another. The executives all know and understand the entire business and can fill in for each other easily on almost any task, whether it's leading a regional celebration, representing the company at a key external event, or kicking off an internal dialogue with employees.

While the behavior of the executive team is crucial to supporting a culture of collaboration, the challenge is to make executives' behavior visible. At Standard

Chartered the senior team travels extensively; the norm is to travel even for relatively brief meetings. This investment in face-to-face interaction creates many opportunities for people across the company to see the top executives in action. Internal communication is frequent and open, and, maybe most telling, every site around the world is filled with photos of groups of executives—country and functional leaders—working together.

The senior team's collaborative nature trickles down throughout the organization. Employees quickly learn that the best way to get things done is through informal networks. For example, when a major program was recently launched to introduce a new customer-facing technology, the team responsible had an almost uncanny ability to understand who the key stakeholders at each branch bank were and how best to approach them. The team members' first-name acquaintance with people across the company brought a sense of dynamism to their interactions.

### Creating a "Gift Culture"

A third important role for executives is to ensure that mentoring and coaching become embedded in their own routine behavior—and throughout the company. We looked at both formal mentoring processes, with clear roles and responsibilities, and less formal processes, where mentoring was integrated into everyday activities. It turned out that while both types were important, the latter was more likely to increase collaborative behavior. Daily coaching helps establish a cooperative "gift culture" in place of a more transactional "tit-for-tat culture."

At Nokia informal mentoring begins as soon as someone steps into a new job. Typically, within a few days, the employee's manager will sit down and list all the people in the organization, no matter in what location, it would be useful for the employee to meet. This is a deeply ingrained cultural norm, which probably originated when Nokia was a smaller and simpler organization. The manager sits with the newcomer, just as her manager sat with her when she joined, and reviews what topics the newcomer should discuss with each person on the list and why establishing a relationship with him or her is important. It is then standard for the newcomer to actively set up meetings with the people on the list, even when it means traveling to other locations. The gift of time—in the form of hours spent on coaching and building networks—is seen as crucial to the collaborative culture at Nokia.

## Focused HR Practices

So what about human resources? Is collaboration solely in the hands of the executive team? In our study we looked at the impact of a wide variety of HR practices, including selection, performance management, promotion, rewards, and training, as well as formally sponsored coaching and mentoring programs.

We found some surprises: for example, that the type of reward system—whether based on team or individual achievement, or tied explicitly to collaborative behavior or not—had no discernible effect on complex teams' productivity and innovation. Although most

# Eight Factors That Lead to Success

1. **Investing in signature relationship practices.** Executives can encourage collaborative behavior by making highly visible investments—in facilities with open floor plans to foster communication, for example—that demonstrate their commitment to collaboration.

2. **Modeling collaborative behavior.** At companies where the senior executives demonstrate highly collaborative behavior themselves, teams collaborate well.

3. **Creating a "gift culture."** Mentoring and coaching—especially on an informal basis—help people build the networks they need to work across corporate boundaries.

4. **Ensuring the requisite skills.** Human resources departments that teach employees how to build relationships, communicate well, and resolve conflicts creatively can have a major impact on team collaboration.

5. **Supporting a strong sense of community.** When people feel a sense of community, they are more comfortable reaching out to others and more likely to share knowledge.

6. **Assigning team leaders that are both task- and relationship-oriented.** The debate has traditionally focused on whether a task or a relationship orientation creates better leadership, but in fact both are key to successfully leading a team. Typically, leaning more heavily on a task orientation at the outset of a project and shifting toward a relationship orientation once the work is in full swing works best.

7. **Building on heritage relationships.** When too many team members are strangers, people may be reluctant to share knowledge. The best practice is to put at least a few people who know one another on the team.

8. **Understanding role clarity and task ambiguity.** Cooperation increases when the roles of individual team members are sharply defined yet the team is given latitude on how to achieve the task.

formal HR programs appeared to have limited impact, we found that two practices did improve team performance: training in skills related to collaborative behavior, and support for informal community building. Where collaboration was strong, the HR team had typically made a significant investment in one or both of those practices—often in ways that uniquely represented the company's culture and business strategy.

### Ensuring the Requisite Skills

Many of the factors that support collaboration relate to what we call the "container" of collaboration—the underlying culture and habits of the company or team. However, we found that some teams had a collaborative culture but were not skilled in the practice of collaboration itself. They were encouraged to cooperate, they wanted to cooperate, but they didn't know how to work together very well in teams.

Our study showed that a number of skills were crucial: appreciating others, being able to engage in purposeful conversations, productively and creatively resolving conflicts, and program management. By training employees in those areas, a company's human resources or corporate learning department can make an important difference in team performance.

In the research, PricewaterhouseCoopers emerged as having one of the strongest capabilities in productive collaboration. With responsibility for developing 140,000 employees in nearly 150 countries, PwC's training includes modules that address teamwork, emotional intelligence, networking, holding difficult conversations,

## How Complex Is the Collaborative Task?

**NOT ALL HIGHLY COLLABORATIVE TASKS** are complex. In assembling and managing a team, consider the project you need to assign and whether the following statements apply:

- The task is unlikely to be accomplished successfully using only the skills within the team.
- The task must be addressed by a new group formed specifically for this purpose.
- The task requires collective input from highly specialized individuals.
- The task requires collective input and agreement from more than 20 people.
- The members of the team working on the task are in more than two locations.
- The success of the task is highly dependent on understanding preferences or needs of individuals outside the group.
- The outcome of the task will be influenced by events that are highly uncertain and difficult to predict.
- The task must be completed under extreme time pressure.

If more than two of these statements are true, the task requires complex collaboration.

---

coaching, corporate social responsibility, and communicating the firm's strategy and shared values. PwC also teaches employees how to influence others effectively and build healthy partnerships.

A number of other successful teams in our sample came from organizations that had a commitment to teaching employees relationship skills. Lehman Brothers' flagship program for its client-facing staff, for instance, is its training in selling and relationship management. The program is not about sales techniques but, rather, focuses on how Lehman values its clients and makes sure that every client has access to all the resources the firm has to offer. It is essentially a course on strategies for building collaborative partnerships with customers, emphasizing the importance of trust-based personal relationships.

**Supporting a Sense of Community**
While a communal spirit can develop spontaneously, we discovered that HR can also play a critical role in cultivating it, by sponsoring group events and activities such as women's networks, cooking weekends, and tennis coaching, or creating policies and practices that encourage them.

At ABN Amro we studied effective change-management teams within the company's enterprise services function. These informal groups were responsible for projects associated with the implementation of new technology throughout the bank; one team, for instance, was charged with expanding online banking services. To succeed, the teams needed the involvement and expertise of different parts of the organization.

The ABN Amro teams rated the company's support for informal communities very positively. The firm makes the technology needed for long-distance collaboration readily available to groups of individuals with shared interests—for instance, in specific technologies or markets—who hold frequent web conferences and communicate actively online. The company also encourages employees that travel to a new location to arrange meetings with as many people as possible. As projects are completed, working groups disband but employees maintain networks of connections. These practices serve to build a strong community over time—one that sets the stage for success with future projects.

Committed investment in informal networks is also a central plank of the HR strategy at Marriott. Despite its size and global reach, Marriott remains a family business, and the chairman, Bill Marriott, makes a point of communicating that idea regularly to employees. He still tells stories of counting sticky nickels at night as a child—proceeds from the root-beer stand founded in downtown Washington, DC, by his mother and father.

Many of the firm's HR investments reinforce a friendly, family-like culture. Almost every communication reflects an element of staff appreciation. A range of "pop-up" events—spontaneous activities—create a sense of fun and community. For example, the cafeteria might roll back to the 1950s, hold a twist dance contest, and in doing so, recognize the anniversary of the company's first hotel opening. Bill Marriott's birthday might be celebrated with parties throughout the company, serving as an occasion to emphasize the firm's culture and values. The chairman recently began his own blog, which is popular with employees, in which he discusses everything from Marriott's efforts to become greener, to his favorite family vacation spots—themes intended to reinforce the idea that the company is a community.

## The Right Team Leaders

In the groups that had high levels of collaborative behavior, the team leaders clearly made a significant difference. The question in our minds was how they actually achieved this. The answer, we saw, lay in their flexibility as managers.

### Assigning Leaders Who Are Both Task- and Relationship-Oriented

There has been much debate among both academics and senior managers about the most appropriate style for leading teams. Some people have suggested that relationship-oriented leadership is most appropriate in complex teams, since people are more likely to share knowledge in an environment of trust and goodwill. Others have argued that a task orientation—the ability to make objectives clear, to create a shared awareness of the dimensions of the task, and to provide monitoring and feedback—is most important.

In the 55 teams we studied, we found that the truth lay somewhere in between. The most productive, innovative teams were typically led by people who were *both* task- and relationship-oriented. What's more, these leaders changed their style during the project. Specifically, at the early stages they exhibited task-oriented leadership: They made the goal clear, engaged in debates about commitments, and clarified the responsibilities of individual team members. However, at a certain point in the development of the project they switched to a relationship orientation. This shift often took place once team members had nailed down the goals and their accountabilities and when the initial tensions around sharing knowledge had begun to emerge. An emphasis throughout a project on one style at the expense of the other inevitably hindered the long-term performance of the team, we found.

Producing ambidextrous team leaders—those with both relationship and task skills—is a core goal of team-leadership development at Marriott. The company's performance-review process emphasizes growth in both kinds of skills. As evidence of their relationship skills, managers are asked to describe their peer network and cite examples of specific ways that network helped them succeed. They also must provide examples of how they've used relationship building to get things done. The development plans that follow these conversations explicitly map out how the managers can improve specific elements of their social relationships and networks. Such a plan might include, for instance, having lunch regularly with people from a particular community of interest.

To improve their task leadership, many people in the teams at Marriott participated in project-management certification programs, taking refresher courses to maintain their skills over time. Evidence of both kinds of capabilities becomes a significant criterion on which people are selected for key leadership roles at the company.

## Team Formation and Structure

The final set of lessons for developing and managing complex teams has to do with the makeup and structure of the teams themselves.

### Building on Heritage Relationships

Given how important trust is to successful collaboration, forming teams that capitalize on preexisting, or "heritage," relationships, increases the chances of a project's success. Our research shows that new teams, particularly those with a high proportion of members who were strangers at the time of formation, find it more difficult to collaborate than those with established relationships.

Newly formed teams are forced to invest significant time and effort in building trusting relationships. However, when some team members already know and trust one another, they can become nodes, which over time evolve into networks. Looking closely at our data, we discovered that when 20% to 40% of the team members were already well connected to one another, the team had strong collaboration right from the start.

It helps, of course, if the company leadership has taken other measures to cultivate networks that cross boundaries. The orientation process at Nokia ensures that a large number of people on any team know one another, increasing the odds that even in a company of more than 100,000 people, someone on a companywide team knows someone else and can make introductions.

Nokia has also developed an organizational architecture designed to make good use of heritage relationships. When it needs to transfer skills across business functions or units, Nokia moves entire small teams intact instead of reshuffling individual people into new positions. If, for example, the company needs to bring together a group of market and technology experts to address a new customer need, the group formed would be composed of small pods of colleagues from each area. This ensures that key heritage relationships continue to strengthen over time, even as the organization redirects its resources to meet market needs. Because the entire company has one common platform for logistics, HR, finance, and other transactions, teams can switch in and out of businesses and geographies without learning new systems.

One important caveat about heritage relationships: If not skillfully managed, too many of them can actually disrupt collaboration. When a significant number of people within the team know one another, they tend to form strong subgroups—whether by function, geography, or anything else they have in common. When that happens, the probability of conflict among the subgroups, which we call fault lines, increases.

### Understanding Role Clarity and Task Ambiguity

Which is more important to promoting collaboration: a clearly defined approach toward achieving the goal, or clearly specified roles for individual team members? The common assumption is that carefully spelling out the approach is essential, but leaving the roles of individuals within the team vague will encourage people to share ideas and contribute in multiple dimensions.

Our research shows that the opposite is true: Collaboration improves when the roles of individual team members are clearly defined and well understood—when individuals feel that they can do a significant portion of their work independently. Without such clarity, team members are likely to waste too much energy negotiating roles or protecting turf, rather than focus on the task. In addition, team members are more likely to want to collaborate if the path to achieving the team's goal is left somewhat ambiguous. If a team perceives the task as one that requires creativity, where the approach is not yet well known or predefined, its members are more likely to invest time and energy in collaboration.

At the BBC we studied the teams responsible for the radio and television broadcasts of the 2006 Proms (a two-month-long musical celebration), the team that televised the 2006 World Cup, and a team responsible for daytime television news. These teams were large— 133 people worked on the Proms, 66 on the World Cup, and 72 on the news—and included members with a wide range of skills and from many disciplines. One would imagine, therefore, that there was a strong possibility of confusion among team members.

To the contrary, we found that the BBC's teams scored among the highest in our sample with regard to the clarity with which members viewed their own roles and the roles of others. Every team was composed of specialists who had deep expertise in their given function, and each person had a clearly defined role. There was little overlap between the responsibilities of the sound technician and the camera operator, and so on. Yet the tasks the BBC teams tackle are, by their very nature, uncertain, particularly when they involve breaking news. The trick the BBC has pulled off has been to clarify team members' individual roles with so much precision that it keeps friction to a minimum.

The successful teams we studied at Reuters worked out of far-flung locations, and often the team members didn't speak a common language. (The primary languages were Russian, Chinese, Thai, and English.) These teams, largely composed of software programmers, were responsible for the rapid development of highly complex technical software and network products. Many of the programmers sat at their desks for 12 hours straight developing code, speaking with no one. Ironically, these teams judged cooperative behavior to be high among their members. That may be because each individual was given autonomy over one discrete piece of the project. The rapid pace and demanding project timelines encouraged individual members to work independently to get the job done, but each person's work had to be shaped with an eye toward the overall team goal.

_____

Strengthening your organization's capacity for collaboration requires a combination of long-term investments—in building relationships and trust, in developing a culture in which senior leaders are role models of cooperation—and smart near-term decisions about the ways teams are formed, roles are defined, and challenges and tasks are articulated. Practices and structures that may have worked well with simple teams of people who were all in one location and knew one another are likely to lead to failure when teams grow more complex.

Most of the factors that impede collaboration today would have impeded collaboration at any time in history. Yesterday's teams, however, didn't require the same amount of members, diversity, long-distance co-operation, or expertise that teams now need to solve global business challenges. So the models for teams need to be realigned with the demands of the current business environment. Through careful attention to the factors we've described in this article, companies can assemble the breadth of expertise needed to solve complex business problems—without inducing the destructive behaviors that can accompany it.

**LYNDA GRATTON** is a professor of management practice at London Business School. **TAMARA J. ERICKSON** is the president of the Concours Institute, the research and education arm of BSG Alliance.

Originally published in November 2007. Reprint R0711F

# Want Collaboration?

Accept—and Actively Manage—Conflict
*by Jeff Weiss and Jonathan Hughes*

**THE CHALLENGE IS A LONG-STANDING** one for senior managers: How do you get people in your organization to work together across internal boundaries? But the question has taken on urgency in today's global and fast-changing business environment. To service multinational accounts, you increasingly need seamless collaboration across geographic boundaries. To improve customer satisfaction, you increasingly need collaboration among functions ranging from R&D to distribution. To offer solutions tailored to customers' needs, you increasingly need collaboration between product and service groups.

Meanwhile, as competitive pressures continually force companies to find ways to do more with less, few managers have the luxury of relying on their own dedicated staffs to accomplish their objectives. Instead, most must work with and through people across the organization, many of whom have different priorities, incentives, and ways of doing things.

Getting collaboration right promises tremendous benefits: a unified face to customers, faster internal decision making, reduced costs through shared resources, and the development of more innovative products. But despite the billions of dollars spent on initiatives to improve collaboration, few companies are happy with the results. Time and again we have seen management teams employ the same few strategies to boost internal cooperation. They restructure their organizations and reengineer their business processes. They create cross-unit incentives. They offer teamwork training. While such initiatives yield the occasional success story, most of them have only limited impact in dismantling organizational silos and fostering collaboration—and many are total failures. (See the sidebar "The Three Myths of Collaboration.")

So what's the problem? Most companies respond to the challenge of improving collaboration in entirely the wrong way. They focus on the symptoms ("Sales and delivery do not work together as closely as they should") rather than on the root cause of failures in cooperation: conflict. The fact is, you can't improve collaboration until you've addressed the issue of conflict.

This can come as a surprise to even the most experienced executives, who generally don't fully appreciate the inevitability of conflict in complex organizations. And even if they do recognize this, many mistakenly assume that efforts to increase collaboration will significantly reduce that conflict, when in fact some of these

# Idea in Brief

Companies try all kinds of ways to improve collaboration among different parts of the organization: cross-unit incentive systems, organizational restructuring, teamwork training. Although these initiatives produce occasional success stories, most have only a limited impact on dismantling organizational silos and fostering collaboration. The problem? Most companies focus on the symptoms ("Sales and delivery do not work together as closely as they should") rather than on the root cause of failures in cooperation: conflict. The fact is, you can't improve collaboration until you've addressed the issue of conflict. The authors offer six strategies for effectively managing conflict: Devise and implement a common method

for resolving conflict; provide people with criteria for making trade-offs; use the escalation of conflict as an opportunity for coaching; establish and enforce a requirement of joint escalation; ensure that managers resolve escalated conflicts directly with their counterparts; and make the process for escalated conflict-resolution transparent. The first three strategies focus on the point of conflict; the second three focus on escalation of conflict up the management chain. Together they constitute a framework for effectively managing discord, one that integrates conflict resolution into day-to-day decision-making processes, thereby removing a barrier to cross-organizational collaboration.

efforts—for example, restructuring initiatives—actually produce more of it.

Executives underestimate not only the inevitability of conflict but also—and this is key—its importance to the organization. The disagreements sparked by differences in perspective, competencies, access to information, and strategic focus within a company actually generate much of the value that can come from collaboration across organizational boundaries. Clashes between parties are

## The Three Myths of Collaboration

Companies attempt to foster collaboration among different parts of their organizations through a variety of methods, many based on a number of seemingly sensible but ultimately misguided assumptions.

### Effective Collaboration Means "Teaming"

Many companies think that teamwork training is the way to promote collaboration across an organization. So they'll get the HR department to run hundreds of managers and their subordinates through intensive two- or three-day training programs. Workshops will offer techniques for getting groups aligned around common goals, for clarifying roles and responsibilities, for operating according to a shared set of behavioral norms, and so on.

Unfortunately, such workshops are usually the right solution to the wrong problems. First, the most critical breakdowns in collaboration typically occur not on actual teams but in the rapid and unstructured interactions between different groups within the organization. For example, someone from R&D will spend weeks unsuccessfully trying to get help from manufacturing to run a few tests on a new prototype. Meanwhile, people in manufacturing begin to complain about arrogant engineers from R&D expecting them to drop everything to help with another one of R&D's pet projects. Clearly, the need for collaboration extends to areas other than a formal team.

The second problem is that breakdowns in collaboration almost always result from fundamental differences among business functions and divisions. Teamwork training offers little guidance on how to work together in the context of competing objectives and limited resources. Indeed, the frequent emphasis on common goals further stigmatizes the idea of conflict in organizations where an emphasis on "polite" behavior regularly prevents effective problem solving. People who need to collaborate more effectively usually don't need to align around and work toward a common goal. They need to quickly and creatively solve problems by managing the inevitable conflict so that it works in their favor.

## An Effective Incentive System Will Ensure Collaboration

It's a tantalizing proposition: You can hardwire collaboration into your organization by rewarding collaborative behavior. Salespeople receive bonuses not only for hitting targets for their own division's products but also for hitting cross-selling targets. Staff in corporate support functions like IT and procurement have part of their bonuses determined by positive feedback from their internal clients.

Unfortunately, the results of such programs are usually disappointing. Despite greater financial incentives, for example, salespeople continue to focus on the sales of their own products to the detriment of selling integrated solutions. Employees continue to perceive the IT and procurement departments as difficult to work with, too focused on their own priorities. Why such poor results? To some extent, it's because individuals think—for the most part correctly—that if they perform well in their own operation they will be "taken care of" by their bosses. In addition, many people find that the costs of working with individuals in other parts of the organization—the extra time required, the aggravation—greatly outweigh the rewards for doing so.

Certainly, misaligned incentives can be a tremendous obstacle to cross-boundary collaboration. But even the most carefully constructed incentives won't eliminate tensions between people with competing business objectives. An incentive is too blunt an instrument to enable optimal resolution of the hundreds of different trade-offs that need to be made in a complex organization. What's more, overemphasis on incentives can create a culture in which people say, "If the company wanted me to do that, they would build it into my comp plan." Ironically, focusing on incentives as a means to encourage collaboration can end up undermining it.

## Organizations Can Be Structured for Collaboration

Many managers look for structural and procedural solutions—cross-functional task forces, collaborative "groupware," complex

*(continued)*

webs of dotted reporting lines on the organization chart—to create greater internal collaboration. But bringing people together is very different from getting them to collaborate.

Consider the following scenario. Individual information technology departments have been stripped out of a company's business units and moved to a corporatewide, shared-services IT organization. Senior managers rightly recognize that this kind of change is a recipe for conflict because various groups will now essentially compete with one another for scarce IT resources. So managers try mightily to design conflict out of, and collaboration into, the new organization. For example, to enable collaborative decision making within IT and between IT and the business units, business units are required to enter requests for IT support into a computerized tracking system. The system is designed to enable managers within the IT organization to prioritize projects and optimally deploy resources to meet the various requests.

Despite painstaking process design, results are disappointing. To avoid the inevitable conflicts between business units and IT over project prioritization, managers in the business units quickly learn to bring their requests to those they know in the IT organization rather than entering the requests into the new system. Consequently, IT professionals assume that any project in the system is a lower priority—further discouraging use of the system. People's inability to deal effectively with conflict has undermined a new process specifically designed to foster organizational collaboration.

---

the crucibles in which creative solutions are developed and wise trade-offs among competing objectives are made. So instead of trying simply to reduce disagreements, senior executives need to embrace conflict and, just as important, institutionalize mechanisms for managing it.

Even though most people lack an innate understanding of how to deal with conflict effectively, there are a number of straightforward ways that executives can help their people—and their organizations—constructively manage it. These can be divided into two main areas: strategies for managing disagreements at the point of conflict and strategies for managing conflict upon escalation up the management chain. These methods can help a company move through the conflict that is a necessary precursor to truly effective collaboration and, more important, extract the value that often lies latent in intra-organizational differences. When companies are able to do both, conflict is transformed from a major liability into a significant asset.

## Strategies for Managing Disagreements at the Point of Conflict

Conflict management works best when the parties involved in a disagreement are equipped to manage it themselves. The aim is to get people to resolve issues on their own through a process that improves—or at least does not damage—their relationships. The following strategies help produce decisions that are better informed and more likely to be implemented.

### Devise and Implement a Common Method for Resolving Conflict

Consider for a moment the hypothetical Matrix Corporation, a composite of many organizations we've worked with whose challenges will likely be familiar to managers. Over the past few years, salespeople from nearly a dozen of Matrix's product and service groups have been called on to design and sell integrated solutions to their customers. For any given sale, five or more lead salespeople and their teams have to agree on issues of resource allocation, solution design, pricing, and sales strategy. Not surprisingly, the teams are finding this difficult. Who should contribute the most resources to a particular customer's offering? Who should reduce the scope of their participation or discount their pricing to meet a customer's budget? Who should defer when disagreements arise about account strategy? Who should manage key relationships within the customer account? Indeed, given these thorny questions, Matrix is finding that a single large sale typically generates far more conflict inside the company than it does with the customer. The resulting wasted time and damaged relationships among sales teams are making it increasingly difficult to close sales.

Most companies face similar sorts of problems. And, like Matrix, they leave employees to find their own ways of resolving them. But without a structured method for dealing with these issues, people get bogged down not only in what the right result should be but also in how to arrive at it. Often, they will avoid or work around conflict, thereby forgoing important opportunities to collaborate. And when people do decide to confront their differences, they usually default to the approach they know best: debating about who's right and who's wrong or haggling over small concessions. Among the negative consequences of such approaches are suboptimal, "split-the-difference" resolutions—if not outright deadlock.

Establishing a companywide process for resolving disagreements can alter this familiar scenario. At the very least, a well-defined, well-designed conflict resolution method will reduce transaction costs, such as wasted time and the accumulation of ill will, that often come with the struggle to work though differences. At best, it will yield the innovative outcomes that are likely to emerge from discussions that draw on a multitude of objectives and perspectives. There is an array of conflict resolution methods a company can use. But to be effective, they should offer a clear, step-by-step process for parties to follow. They should also be made an integral part of existing business activities—account planning, sourcing, R&D budgeting, and the like. If conflict resolution is set up as a separate, exception-based process— a kind of organizational appeals court—it will likely wither away once initial managerial enthusiasm wanes.

At Intel, new employees learn a common method and language for decision making and conflict resolution. The company puts them through training in which they learn to use a variety of tools for handling discord. Not only does the training show that top management sees disagreements as an inevitable aspect of doing business, it also provides a common framework that expedites conflict resolution. Little time is wasted in figuring out the best way to handle a disagreement or trading accusations about "not being a team player"; guided by this clearly defined process, people can devote their time and energy to exploring and constructively evaluating a variety of options for how to move forward. Intel's systematic method for working through differences has helped sustain some of the company's hallmark qualities: innovation, operational efficiency, and the ability to make and implement hard decisions in the face of complex strategic choices.

### Provide People With Criteria for Making Trade-Offs

At our hypothetical Matrix Corporation, senior managers overseeing cross-unit sales teams often admonish those teams to "do what's right for the customer." Unfortunately, this exhortation isn't much help when conflict arises. Given Matrix's ability to offer numerous combinations of products and services, company managers—each with different training and experience and access to different information, not to mention different unit priorities—have, not surprisingly, different opinions about how best to meet customers' needs. Similar clashes in perspective result when exasperated senior managers tell squabbling team members to set aside their differences and "put Matrix's interests first." That's because it isn't always clear what's best for the company given the complex interplay among Matrix's objectives for revenue, profitability, market share, and long-term growth.

Even when companies equip people with a common method for resolving conflict, employees often will still need to make zero-sum trade-offs between competing priorities. That task is made much easier and less contentious when top management can clearly articulate the criteria for making such choices. Obviously, it's not easy to reduce a company's strategy to clearly defined trade-offs, but it's worth trying. For example, salespeople who know that five points of market share are more important than a ten point increase on a customer satisfaction scale are much better equipped to make strategic concessions when the needs and priorities of different parts of the business conflict. And even when the criteria do not lead to a straightforward answer, the guidelines can at least foster productive conversations by providing an objective focus. Establishing such criteria also sends a clear signal from management that it views conflict as an inevitable result of managing a complex business.

At Blue Cross and Blue Shield of Florida, the strategic decision to rely more and more on alliances with other organizations has significantly increased the potential for disagreement in an organization long accustomed to developing capabilities in-house. Decisions about whether to build new capabilities, buy them outright, or gain access to them through alliances are natural flashpoints for conflict among internal groups. The health insurer might have tried to minimize such conflict through a structural solution, giving a particular group the authority to make decisions concerning whether, for instance, to develop a new claims-processing system in-house, to do so jointly with an alliance partner, or to license or acquire an existing system from a third party. Instead, the company established a set of criteria designed to help various groups within the organization—for example, the enterprise alliance group, IT, and marketing—to collectively make such decisions.

## Blue Cross and Blue Shield: build, buy, or ally?

*One of the most effective ways senior managers can help resolve cross-unit conflict is by giving people the criteria for making trade-offs when the needs of different parts of the business are at odds with one another. At Blue Cross and Blue Shield of Florida, there are often conflicting perspectives over whether to build new capabilities (for example, a new claims-processing system, as in the hypothetical example below), acquire them, or gain access to them through an alliance. The company uses a grid-like poster (a simplified version of which is shown here) that helps multiple parties analyze the trade-offs associated with these three options. By checking various boxes in the grid using personalized markers, participants indicate how they assess a particular option against a variety of criteria: for example, the date by which the new capability needs to be implemented; the availability of internal resources such as capital and staff needed to develop the capability; and the degree of integration required with existing products and processes. The table format makes criteria and trade-offs easy to compare. The visual depiction of people's "votes" and the ensuing discussion help individuals see how their differences often arise from such factors as access to different data or different prioritizing of objectives. As debate unfolds—and as people move their markers in response to new information—they can see where they are aligned and where and why they separate into significant factions of disagreement. Eventually, the criteria-based dialogue tends to produce a preponderance of markers in one of the three rows, thus yielding operational consensus around a decision.*

**New claims-processing system**

| Required implementation time frame | Organizational experience level | Availability of internal resources | Volatility of environment | Complexity of solution | Availability of external resources | Required degree of integration | Required control | |
|---|---|---|---|---|---|---|---|---|
| >12 months | High | High | Low | Low | Low | High | High | Build |
| <6 months | Low | High to moderate | Medium | High | High | Medium | Medium | Buy |
| 6–12 months | Medium | Moderate to low | High | Moderate | Moderate | Low | Low | Ally |

Participant 1 = √   Participant 2 = √   Participant 3 = ☆   Participant 4 = ✗   Participant 5 = ✗

Source: Blue Cross and Blue Shield of Florida.

The criteria are embodied in a spreadsheet-type tool that guides people in assessing the trade-offs involved—say, between speed in getting a new process up and running versus ensuring its seamless integration with existing ones—when deciding whether to build, buy, or ally. People no longer debate back and forth across a table, advocating their preferred outcomes. Instead, they sit around the table and together apply a common set of trade-off criteria to the decision at hand. The resulting insights into the pros and cons of each approach enable more effective execution, no matter which path is chosen. (For a simplified version of the trade-off tool, see the exhibit "Blue Cross and Blue Shield: build, buy, or ally?")

### Use the Escalation of Conflict as an Opportunity for Coaching

Managers at Matrix spend much of their time playing the organizational equivalent of hot potato. Even people who are new to the company learn within weeks that the best thing to do with cross-unit conflict is to toss it up the management chain. Immediate supervisors take a quick pass at resolving the dispute but, being busy themselves, usually pass it up to *their* supervisors. Those supervisors do the same, and before long the problem lands in the lap of a senior-level manager, who then spends much of his time resolving disagreements. Clearly, this isn't ideal. Because the senior managers are a number of steps removed from the source of the controversy, they rarely have a good understanding of the situation. Furthermore, the more time they spend resolving internal clashes, the less time they spend engaged in the business, and the more isolated they are from the very information they need to resolve the disputes dumped in their laps. Meanwhile, Matrix employees get so little opportunity to learn about how to deal with conflict that it becomes not only expedient but almost necessary for them to quickly bump conflict up the management chain.

While Matrix's story may sound extreme, we can hardly count the number of companies we've seen that operate this way. And even in the best of situations—for example, where a companywide conflict-management process is in place and where trade-off criteria are well understood—there is still a natural tendency for people to let their bosses sort out disputes. Senior managers contribute to this tendency by quickly resolving the problems presented to them. While this may be the fastest and easiest way to fix the problems, it encourages people to punt issues upstairs at the first sign of difficulty. Instead, managers should treat escalations as opportunities to help employees become better at resolving conflict. (For an example of how managers can help their employees improve their conflict resolution skills, see the exhibit "IBM: coaching for conflict.")

At KLA-Tencor, a major manufacturer of semiconductor production equipment, a materials executive in each division oversees a number of buyers who procure the materials and component parts for machines that the division makes. When negotiating a companywide contract with a supplier, a buyer often must work with the company commodity manager, as well as with buyers

## IBM: coaching for conflict

*Managers can reduce the repeated escalation of conflict up the management chain by helping employees learn how to resolve disputes themselves. At IBM, executives get training in conflict management and are offered online resources to help them coach others. One tool on the corporate intranet (an edited excerpt of which is shown here) walks managers through a variety of conversations they might have with a direct report who is struggling to resolve a dispute with people from one or more groups in the company—some of whom, by design, will be consulted to get their views but won't be involved in negotiating the final decision.*

| If you hear from someone reporting to you that ... | The problem could be that ... | And you could help your report by saying something like... |
| --- | --- | --- |
| "Everyone still insists on being a decision maker." | The people your report is dealing with remain concerned that unless they have a formal voice in making the decision—or a key piece of the decision—their needs and interests won't be taken into account. | "You might want to explain why people are being consulted and how this information will be used." "Are there ways to break this decision apart into a series of sub-issues and assign decision-making roles around those subissues?" "Consider talking to the group about the costs of having everyone involved in the final decision." |
| "If I consult with this person up front, he might try to force an answer on me or create roadblocks to my efforts to move forward." | The person you are coaching may be overlooking the risks of not asking for input—mainly, that any decision arrived at without input could be sabotaged later on. | "How would you ask someone for input? What would you tell her about your purpose in seeking it? What questions would you ask? What would you say if she put forth a solution and resisted discussing other options?" "Is there a way to manage the risk that she will try to block your efforts other than by not consulting her at all? If you consult with her now, might that in fact lower the risk that she will try to derail your efforts later?" |
| "I have consulted with all the right parties and have crafted, by all accounts, a good plan. But the decision makers cannot settle on a final decision." | The right people were included in the negotiating group, but the process for negotiating a final decision was not determined. | "What are the ground rules for how decisions will be made? Do all those in the group need to agree? Must the majority agree? Or just those with the greatest competence?" "What interests underlie the objective of having everyone agree? Is there another decision-making process that would meet those interests?" |

from other divisions who deal with the same supplier. There is often conflict, for example, over the delivery terms for components supplied to two or more divisions under the contract. In such cases, the commodity manager and the division materials executive will push the division buyer to consider the needs of the other divisions, alternatives that might best address the collective needs of the different divisions, and the standards to be applied in assessing the trade-offs between alternatives. The aim is to help the buyer see solutions that haven't yet been considered and to resolve the conflict with the buyer in the other division.

Initially, this approach required more time from managers than if they had simply made the decisions themselves. But it has paid off in fewer disputes that senior managers need to resolve, speedier contract negotiation, and improved contract terms both for the company as a whole and for multiple divisions. For example, the buyers from three KLA-Tencor product divisions recently locked horns over a global contract with a key supplier. At issue was the trade-off between two variables: one, the supplier's level of liability for materials it needs to purchase in order to fulfill orders and, two, the flexibility granted the KLA-Tencor divisions in modifying the size of the orders and their required lead times. Each division demanded a different balance between these two factors, and the buyers took the conflict to their managers, wondering if they should try to negotiate each of the different trade-offs into the contract or pick among them. After being coached to consider how each division's business model shaped its preference—and using this understanding to jointly brainstorm alternatives—the buyers and commodity manager arrived at a creative solution that worked for everyone: They would request a clause in the contract that allowed them to increase and decrease flexibility in order volume and lead time, with corresponding changes in supplier liability, as required by changing market conditions.

## Strategies for Managing Conflict upon Escalation

Equipped with common conflict resolution methods and trade-off criteria, and supported by systematic coaching, people are better able to resolve conflict on their own. But certain complex disputes will inevitably need to be decided by superiors. Consequently, managers must ensure that, upon escalation, conflict is resolved constructively and efficiently—and in ways that model desired behaviors.

### Establish and Enforce a Requirement of Joint Escalation

Let's again consider the situation at Matrix. In a typical conflict, three salespeople from different divisions become involved in a dispute over pricing. Frustrated, one of them decides to hand the problem up to his boss, explaining the situation in a short voice-mail message. The message offers little more than bare acknowledgment of the other salespeoples' viewpoints. The manager then determines, on the basis of what he knows about the situation, the solution to the problem. The salesperson, armed with his boss's decision, returns to his counterparts and shares with them the verdict— which, given the process, is simply a stronger version of the solution the salesperson had put forward in the first place. But wait! The other two salespeople have also gone to *their* managers and carried back stronger versions of *their* solutions. At this point, each salesperson is locked into what is now "my manager's view" of the right pricing scheme. The problem, already thorny, has become even more intractable.

The best way to avoid this kind of debilitating deadlock is for people to present a disagreement jointly to their boss or bosses. This will reduce or even eliminate the suspicion, surprises, and damaged personal relationships ordinarily associated with unilateral escalation. It will also guarantee that the ultimate decision maker has access to a wide array of perspectives on the conflict, its causes, and the various ways it might be resolved. Furthermore, companies that require people to share responsibility for the escalation of a conflict often see a decrease in the number of problems that are pushed up the management chain. Joint escalation helps create the kind of accountability that is lacking when people know they can provide their side of an issue to their own manager and blame others when things don't work out.

A few years ago, after a merger that resulted in a much larger and more complex organization, senior managers at the Canadian telecommunications company Telus found themselves virtually paralyzed by a daily barrage of unilateral escalations. Just determining who was dealing with what and who should be talking to whom took up huge amounts of senior management's time. So the company made joint escalation a central tenet of its new organizationwide protocols for conflict resolution—a requirement given teeth by managers' refusal to respond to unilateral escalation. When a conflict occurred among managers in different departments concerning, say, the allocation of resources among the departments, the managers were required to jointly describe the problem, what had been done so far to resolve it, and its possible solutions. Then they had to send a joint write-up of the situation to each of their bosses and stand ready to appear together and answer questions when those bosses met to work through a solution. In many cases, the requirement of systematically documenting the conflict and efforts to resolve it—because it forced people to make such efforts—led to a problem being resolved on the spot, without having to be kicked upstairs. Within weeks, this process resulted in the resolution of hundreds of issues that had been stalled for months in the newly merged organization.

### Ensure That Managers Resolve Escalated Conflicts Directly with *Their* Counterparts

Let's return to the three salespeople at Matrix who took their dispute over pricing to their respective bosses and then met again, only to find themselves further from agreement than before. So what did they do at that point? They sent the problem *back* to their bosses. These three bosses, each of whom thought he'd already resolved the issue, decided the easiest thing to do would be to escalate it themselves. This would save them time and put the conflict before senior managers with the broad view seemingly needed to make a decision. Unfortunately, by doing this, the three bosses simply perpetuated the situation their salespeople had created, putting forward a biased viewpoint and leaving it to their own managers to come up with an answer. In the end, the decision was made unilaterally by the senior manager with the most organizational clout. This result bred resentment back down the management chain. A sense of "we'll win next time" took hold, ensuring that future conflict would be even more difficult to resolve.

It's not unusual to see managers react to escalations from their employees by simply passing conflicts up their own functional or divisional chains until they reach a senior executive involved with all the affected functions or divisions. Besides providing a poor example for others in the organization, this can be disastrous for a company that needs to move quickly. To avoid wasting time, a manager somewhere along the chain might try to resolve the problem swiftly and decisively by herself. But this, too, has its costs. In a complex organization, where many issues have significant implications for numerous parts of the business, unilateral responses to unilateral escalations are a recipe for inefficiency, bad decisions, and ill feelings.

The solution to these problems is a commitment by managers—a commitment codified in a formal policy— to deal with escalated conflict directly with their counterparts. Of course, doing this can feel cumbersome, especially when an issue is time-sensitive. But resolving the problem early on is ultimately more efficient than trying to sort it out later, after a decision becomes known because it has negatively affected some part of the business.

In the 1990s, IBM's sales and delivery organization became increasingly complex as the company reintegrated previously independent divisions and reorganized itself to provide customers with full solutions of bundled products and services. Senior executives soon recognized that managers were not dealing with escalated conflicts and that relationships among them were strained because they failed to consult and coordinate around cross-unit issues. This led to the creation of a forum called the Market Growth Workshop (a name carefully chosen to send a message throughout the company that getting cross-unit conflict resolved was critical to meeting customer needs and, in turn, growing market share). These monthly conference calls brought together managers, salespeople, and frontline product specialists from across the company to discuss and resolve cross-unit conflicts that were hindering important sales—for example, the difficulty salespeople faced in getting needed technical resources from overstretched product groups.

The Market Growth Workshops weren't successful right away. In the beginning, busy senior managers, reluctant to spend time on issues that often hadn't been carefully thought through, began sending their subordinates to the meetings—which made it even more difficult to resolve the problems discussed. So the company developed a simple preparation template that forced people to document and analyze disputes before the conference calls. Senior managers, realizing the problems created by their absence, recommitted themselves to attending the meetings. Over time, as complex conflicts were resolved during these sessions and significant sales were closed, attendees began to see these meetings as an opportunity to be involved in the resolution of high-stakes, high-visibility issues.

## Make the Process for Escalated Conflict Resolution Transparent

When a sales conflict is resolved by a Matrix senior manager, the word comes down the management chain in the form of an action item: Put together an offering with this particular mix of products and services at these prices. The only elaboration may be an admonishment to "get the sales team together, work up a proposal, and get back to the customer as quickly as possible." The problem is solved, at least for the time being. But the salespeople—unless they have been able to divine themes from the patterns of decisions made over time— are left with little guidance on how to resolve similar issues in the future. They may justifiably wonder: How was the decision made? Based on what kinds of assumptions? With what kinds of trade-offs? How might the reasoning change if the situation were different?

In most companies, once managers have resolved a conflict, they announce the decision and move on. The resolution process and rationale behind the decision are left inside a managerial black box. While it's rarely helpful for managers to share all the gory details of their deliberations around contentious issues, failing to take the time to explain how a decision was reached and the factors that went into it squanders a major opportunity. A frank discussion of the trade-offs involved in decisions would provide guidance to people trying to resolve conflicts in the future and would help nip in the bud the kind of speculation—who won and who lost, which managers or units have the most power—that breeds mistrust, sparks turf battles, and otherwise impedes cross-organizational collaboration. In general, clear communication about the resolution of the conflict can increase people's willingness and ability to implement decisions.

During the past two years, IBM's Market Growth Workshops have evolved into a more structured approach to managing escalated conflict, known as Cross-Team Workouts. Designed to make conflict resolution more transparent, the workouts are weekly meetings of people across the organization who work together on sales and delivery issues for specific accounts. The meetings provide a public forum for resolving conflicts over account strategy, solution configuration, pricing, and delivery. Those issues that cannot be resolved at the local level are escalated to regional workout sessions attended by managers from product groups, services, sales, and finance. Attendees then communicate and explain meeting resolutions to their reports. Issues that cannot be resolved at the regional level are escalated to an even higher-level workout meeting attended by cross-unit executives from a larger geographic region—like the Americas or Asia

Pacific—and chaired by the general manager of the region presenting the issue. The most complex and strategic issues reach this global forum. The overlapping attendance at these sessions—in which the managers who chair one level of meeting attend sessions at the next level up, thereby observing the decision-making process at that stage—further enhances the transparency of the system among different levels of the company. IBM has further formalized the process for the direct resolution of conflicts between services and product sales on large accounts by designating a managing director in sales and a global relationship partner in IBM global services as the ultimate point of resolution for escalated conflicts. By explicitly making the resolution of complex conflicts part of the job descriptions for both managing director and global relationship partner—and by making that clear to others in the organization—IBM has reduced ambiguity, increased transparency, and increased the efficiency with which conflicts are resolved.

## Tapping the Learning Latent in Conflict

The six strategies we have discussed constitute a framework for effectively managing organizational discord, one that integrates conflict resolution into day-to-day decision-making processes, thereby removing a critical barrier to cross-organizational collaboration. But the strategies also hint at something else: that conflict can be more than a necessary antecedent to collaboration.

Let's return briefly to Matrix. More than three-quarters of all cross-unit sales at the company trigger disputes about pricing. Roughly half of the sales lead to clashes over account control. A substantial number of sales also produce disagreements over the design of customer solutions, with the conflict often rooted in divisions' incompatible measurement systems and the concerns of some people about the quality of the solutions being assembled. But managers are so busy trying to resolve these almost daily disputes that they don't see the patterns or sources of conflict. Interestingly, if they ever wanted to identify patterns like these, Matrix managers might find few signs of them. That's because salespeople, who regularly hear their bosses complain about all the disagreements in the organization, have concluded that they'd better start shielding their superiors from discord.

The situation at Matrix is not unusual—most companies view conflict as an unnecessary nuisance—but that view is unfortunate. When a company begins to see conflict as a valuable resource that should be managed and exploited, it is likely to gain insight into problems that senior managers may not have known existed. Because internal friction is often caused by unaddressed strains within an organization or between an organization and its environment, setting up methods to track conflict and examine its causes can provide an interesting new perspective on a variety of issues. In the case of Matrix, taking the time to aggregate the experiences of individual salespeople involved in recurring disputes would likely lead to better approaches to setting prices, establishing incentives for salespeople, and monitoring the company's quality control process.

At Johnson & Johnson, an organization that has a highly decentralized structure, conflict is recognized as a positive aspect of cross-company collaboration. For example, a small internal group charged with facilitating sourcing collaboration among J&J's independent operating companies—particularly their outsourcing of clinical research services—actively works to extract lessons from conflicts. The group tracks and analyzes disagreements about issues such as what to outsource, whether and how to shift spending among suppliers, and what supplier capabilities to invest in. It hosts a council, comprising representatives from the various operating companies, that meets regularly to discuss these differences and explore their strategic implications. As a result, trends in clinical research outsourcing are spotted and information about them is disseminated throughout J&J more quickly. The operating companies benefit from insights about new offshoring opportunities, technologies, and ways of structuring collaboration with suppliers. And J&J, which can now piece together an accurate and global view of its suppliers, is better able to partner with them. Furthermore, the company realizes more value from its relationship with suppliers—yet another example of how the effective management of conflict can ultimately lead to fruitful collaboration.

J&J's approach is unusual but not unique. The benefits it offers provide further evidence that conflict—so often viewed as a liability to be avoided whenever possible—can be valuable to a company that knows how to manage it.

**JEFF WEISS** heads the Alliance Management Practice at Vantage Partners in Boston. **JONATHAN HUGHES** heads the firm's Sourcing and Supplier Management Practice. The authors have had consulting relationships with a number of the companies mentioned in this article.

Originally published in March 2005. Reprint R0503F

# Silo Busting

How to Execute on the Promise of
Customer Focus
*by Ranjay Gulati*

**IN 2001, UNDER PRICE** pressure from the government
and managed health care organizations, GE Medical
Systems (now GE Healthcare) created a unit, Performance Solutions, to sell consulting services packaged
with imaging equipment as integrated solutions. These
solutions, priced at a premium, were intended to enhance productivity by, for instance, reducing patient
backlogs. At the time, lots of companies were making
the move from selling products to selling solutions in an
attempt to differentiate themselves in increasingly
commoditized markets.

GE's plan seemed to work well at first. The Performance Solutions unit enjoyed strong initial revenues, in
part because most new contracts included additional
consulting services valued at $25,000 to $50,000. And
the unit had some notable successes. It helped Stanford
University Medical Center, for example, make the tran-
sition to an all-digital imaging environment at its adult

hospital, children's medical center, and an outpatient facility—moves that delivered millions of dollars in new revenues for the medical center and substantial cost savings.

But by 2005, the unit's growth had begun a swift decline. It turned out that equipment salespeople had trouble explaining the value of consulting services, so when they called on customers they couldn't contribute much to the sale of additional services. What's more, these reps were reluctant to allow Performance Solutions salespeople to contact their customers. And by marketing the unit's consulting services with its product portfolio, GE generated solutions that were useful for customers whose problems could clearly be solved using GE's equipment but less compelling for those whose needs were linked only loosely to the imaging products.

In the end, GE refashioned the unit to address customers' needs in a more comprehensive fashion and to better align the sales organization. For instance, the majority of solutions now focus mainly on consulting services and are no longer marketed only with GE equipment. The solutions group secured new contracts valued at more than $500 million in 2006. But in trying to escape the perils of commoditization, the company initially fell into a classic trap: It was seeking to solve customer problems but was viewing those problems through the lens of its own products, rather than from the customer's perspective. It was pulling together what it had on offer in the hope that customers would value the whole more than the sum of its parts.

# Idea in Brief

For many senior executives, shifting from selling products to selling solutions—packages of products and services—is a priority in today's increasingly commoditized markets. Companies, however, aren't always structured to make that shift. Knowledge and expertise often reside in silos, and many companies have trouble harnessing their resources across those boundaries in a way that customers value and are willing to pay for. Some companies—like GE Healthcare, Best Buy, and commercial real estate provider Jones Lang LaSalle (JLL)—have restructured themselves around customer needs to deliver true solutions. They did so by engaging in four sets of activities. **Coordination**—to deliver customer-focused solutions, three things must occur easily across boundaries: information sharing, division of labor, and decision making. Sometimes this involves replacing traditional silos with customer-focused ones, but more often it entails transcending existing boundaries. JLL has experimented with both approaches. **Cooperation**—customer-centric companies, such as Cisco Systems, develop metrics for customer satisfaction and incentives that reward customer-focused cooperation. Most also shake up the power structure so that people who are closest to customers have the authority to act on their behalf. **Capability**—delivering customer-focused solutions requires some employees to be generalists instead of specialists. They need experience with more than one product or service, a deep knowledge of customer needs, and the ability to traverse internal boundaries. **Connection**—by combining their offerings with those of a partner, companies can cut costs even as they create higher-value solutions, as Starbucks has found through its diverse partnerships. To stand out in a commoditized market, companies must understand what customers value. Ultimately, some customers may be better off purchasing products and services piecemeal.

Over the past five years, I have studied the challenge of top- and bottom-line growth in the face of commoditization, and I have found that many companies make the same mistake. They profess the importance of shifting from products to solutions—in fact, in a survey of senior executives I conducted a few years ago, more than two-thirds of the respondents cited this shift as a strategic priority in the next decade. But their knowledge and expertise are housed within organizational silos, and they have trouble harnessing their resources across those internal boundaries in a way that customers truly value and are willing to pay for.

Some notable exceptions have emerged: companies that, like GE, found ways to transcend those silos in the interest of customer needs. By the late 1990s, for instance, Best Buy had nearly saturated the market with store openings and was facing increased competition not just from other retailers like Wal-Mart but from suppliers such as Dell. It tried to spark growth through various marketing approaches, but the company's efforts didn't take off until it launched a major initiative to restructure around customer solutions. Between 2000 and 2005, Best Buy's stock price grew at an annual rate of almost 30%.

Commercial real estate provider Jones Lang LaSalle (JLL), under serious price competition, made a similar strategic shift in 2001, when its large customers began demanding integrated real estate services. For instance, corporate customers wanted the same people who found or built property for them to manage it. In response, JLL adopted a solutions-oriented structure that helped attract numerous large and highly profitable new accounts.

For GE Healthcare, Best Buy, and JLL, as well as for other companies I have studied, the journey to understand and unite around customer needs was a multiyear endeavor with major challenges and setbacks along the way. The effort required systematic, ongoing change to help organizations transcend existing product-based or geographic silos and, in some cases, replace them with customer-oriented ones. In particular, I found that successful companies engaged in four sets of activities:

**Coordination.** Establishing structural mechanisms and processes that allow employees to improve their focus on the customer by harmonizing information and activities across units.

**Cooperation.** Encouraging people in all parts of the company—through cultural means, incentives, and the allocation of power—to work together in the interest of customer needs.

**Capability development.** Ensuring that enough people in the organization have the skills to deliver customer-focused solutions and defining a clear career path for employees with those skills.

**Connection.** Developing relationships with external partners to increase the value of solutions cost effectively.

The first three sets of activities mutually reinforce the effort to put customers at the organization's fore; the fourth dramatically increases the power and reach of solutions by focusing attention beyond the firm's boundaries. All of them help companies transcend internal silos in service of higher-value customer solutions.

## Coordination for Customer Focus

As GE Healthcare quickly discovered, it's easy to say that you offer solutions; salespeople may readily seize the concept as their newest product. But I've found that few companies are actually structured to deliver products and services in a synchronized way that's attractive from a customer's perspective. Individual units are historically focused on perfecting their products and processes, and give little thought to how their offerings might be even more valuable to the end user when paired with those of another unit. It's not just that the status quo doesn't reward collaborative behavior— although the right incentives are also critical. It's that the connections literally aren't in place.

One way to forge those connections is to do away with traditional silos altogether and create new ones organized by customer segments or needs. Many companies, however, are understandably reluctant to let go of the economies of scale and depth of knowledge and expertise associated with non-customer-focused silos. A company organized around geographies can customize offerings to suit local preferences, for instance, while a technology-centric firm can be quick to market with technical innovations. In many cases, functional and geographic silos were created precisely to help companies coordinate such activities as designing innovative products or gaining geographic focus. A customer focus requires them to emphasize a different set of activities and coordinate them in a different way.

In their initial attempts to offer customer solutions, companies are likely to create structures and processes that transcend rather than obliterate silos. Such boundary-spanning efforts may be highly informal—even as simple as hoping for or encouraging serendipity and impromptu conversations that lead to unplanned cross-unit solutions. But the casual exchange of information and ideas is generally most effective among senior executives, who have a better understanding than their subordinates of corporate goals and easier access to other leaders in the organization.

One way to achieve more-formal coordination without discarding existing silos is to layer boundary-spanning roles or units over the current structure and charge them with connecting the company's disparate activities to customer needs. JLL, which was created by the 1999 merger of LaSalle Partners and Jones Lang Wootton, had organized the corporate side of its business in the Americas into three units, each offering a particular service: representing tenants who wished to lease or purchase, maintaining buildings and properties, and managing real estate development. Each unit had authority over what services to offer, at what price, and to which clients. The units also had profit-and-loss responsibility for their respective businesses.

In 2001 the firm began to hear complaints from such large corporate clients as Bank of America that buying real estate services piecemeal from numerous companies and interacting with relatively junior sales people

# The Four Cs of Customer-Focused Solutions

**COMPANIES LOOKING TO GROW** in a commoditized marketplace like to say that they offer customer solutions: strategic packages of products and services that are hard to copy and can command premium prices. But most companies aren't set up to deliver solutions that customers truly value. Successful companies make significant changes in four areas to deliver real solutions.

## Coordination

In most companies, knowledge and expertise reside in distinct units—organized by product, service, or geography. To deliver customer-focused solutions, companies need mechanisms that allow customer-related information sharing, division of labor, and decision making to occur easily across company boundaries. Sometimes this involves completely obliterating established silos and replacing them with silos organized around the customer, but more often it entails using structures and processes to transcend existing boundaries.

## Cooperation

Customer-centric companies use both substance and symbolism to foster a culture of customer-focused cooperation. They develop metrics that measure, for instance, customer satisfaction and incentives that reward customer-focused behavior, even if it sacrifices unit performance. Most also shake up the power structure so

were taking up too much executive time. One client explained, "We like him [the ad hoc account manager], but he is too low on the totem pole." At the time, many *Fortune* 500 companies were starting to outsource all real estate management. In response, JLL created an umbrella group, Corporate Solutions, that comprised that people who are closest to customers have the authority to act on their behalf.

## Capability

Delivering customer-focused solutions requires at least some employees to have two kinds of generalist skills. The first is experience with more than one product or service, along with a deep knowledge of customer needs (multidomain skills), and the second is an ability to traverse internal boundaries (boundary-spanning skills). In many companies, especially those organized around products, employees aren't rewarded for being generalists. Organizations that succeed in delivering solutions, however, invest significant time and resources in developing generalists. Furthermore, they establish clear career pathways for those who pursue the generalist route.

## Connection

By redefining the boundaries of the company in order to connect more tightly with external partners, companies can not only cut costs by outsourcing all but core activities (and perhaps even by finding ways to outsource them) but also create higher-value solutions by combining their offerings with those of a complementary partner. Working with other companies still means crossing boundaries, but in this instance the boundaries are between a company and its partners.

---

the three service units as well as an account management function, which served as a point of contact for large corporate customers. The account management group was staffed with high-ranking officers who had the authority to negotiate the pricing and delivery of real estate solutions, and the experience to help clients with strategic planning. By approaching Bank of America with a dedicated, senior-level account manager, JLL addressed the customer's complaint and was rewarded with one of just two spots (reduced from five) as a provider of outsourced services for the bank's 65 million square feet of U.S. real estate. Thus began a tremendous run that saw JLL's solutions revenue in the Americas grow more than 50% between 2002 and 2005.

Cisco Systems took a similar, layered approach to customer focus, but with a twist. The company, which had been organized by customer segment from 1997 to 2001, reverted to a technology-focused structure after the Internet bubble burst, forcing the company to address costly redundancies. Under its previous structure, Cisco had been creating the same or similar products for different customer segments, whose needs often overlapped. In fact, in some cases each line of business offered its own technology or solution for the same problem.

However, leaders feared that organizing around technologies, which involved centralizing marketing and R&D, would distance Cisco from customers' requirements. The answer was to retain the company's three sales groups based on customer type but establish a central marketing organization—residing between the technology groups and the customer-facing sales units—responsible for, among other things, facilitating the integration of products and technologies. The marketing group also established a cross-silo solutions-engineering team to bring disparate technologies together in a lab, test them, and create blueprints for end-user solutions. In addition to those structural measures, Cisco implemented several customer-focused processes, such as a customer champion program, which assigned senior executives as advocates for important customers. CEO John Chambers, for instance, was designated Ford's champion in 2002. In 2004 the company supplemented its advocates with cross-functional leadership teams organized by customer type, mimicking the previous structure, at least at the senior management level. Those teams—described by one executive as "the voice of the customer"—oversee six end-to-end processes that cut across functional boundaries such as quote-to-cash (the order cycle) and issue-to-resolution (technical support).

While bridging mechanisms such as cross-silo teams and processes can be very effective, they aren't easy to implement. A history of independence often leads to protectionist behavior. At JLL, for instance, business unit managers were initially reluctant to cede decision-making authority to account managers, particularly ones who lacked experience with that unit's service. Conflicts also arose over pricing and account managers' compensation. What's more, while JLL's Corporate Solutions group had positioned the firm well to meet the increasing demands of corporate real estate customers, single-transaction customers considered the relatively small number of JLL account managers in local markets to be a problem. Those customers wanted professionals who could negotiate the best deal and execute entire transactions. As JLL discovered, the benefits of bundled solutions wear off if customers perceive a weakness in any component. Ultimately, JLL's layered approach to silo busting was still limiting the firm's growth.

To dispense with such tensions, JLL next took the more dramatic and highly formal measure of silo swapping—a wholesale, permanent structural shift to spin internal groups and processes around a customer axis. That is, it swapped its current, service-focused silos for those structured explicitly around the customer to maximize company-customer synergies. As part of that process, it replaced the account management function and the three service silos that had resided within the Corporate Solutions group with two organizations denoted simply Clients and Markets, a restructuring that put more people in the field, closer to clients, and focused all internal groups and processes on customer needs. The Markets organization handled one-off transactions, represented JLL's full range of offerings to those customers, and provided local support for larger clients. As accounts grew, they were assigned an account manager from the Clients organization, which was composed primarily of account teams managing the firm's relationships with large, multiservice customers. These teams were considered profit centers and so had the authority to hire and terminate employees. To preserve its product and service expertise without a product- and service-based structure, JLL embedded service specialists within account teams in both organizations and created a product management team charged with keeping offerings competitive. It's too soon to know how well the customer-focused silos are working, and the firm may face new, unanticipated challenges, but early results look promising: In the past year, revenues have increased by 30% and profits by almost 60%.

## Culture of Cooperation

While coordination mechanisms can align tasks and information around customers' needs, they don't necessarily inspire a willingness among members of competing silos to fully cooperate and make sometimes time-consuming and costly adjustments in the interest of customers. Just as important as coordination, then, is a cooperative environment in which people are rewarded for busting through silos to deliver customer solutions. Customer-centric companies live by a set of values that put the customer front and center, and they reinforce those values through cultural elements, power structures, metrics, and incentives that reward customer-focused, solutions-oriented behavior.

Many product-centric companies probably start out with a focus on customers, aiming to design products with broad appeal. But after early successes, they internalize and institutionalize the notion that markets respond primarily to great products and services. Decisions and behaviors, including those related specifically to customers, are then viewed through the lens of the product. Quality, for example, is defined by meeting internal standards rather than customer requirements. Over time, even the sales and marketing departments lose their customer focus, as product successes dominate company lore. In this way, the company develops a pervasive inside-out perspective.

In contrast, customer-focused companies, even those in technology-intensive arenas, build an outside-in perspective into all major elements of their cultures. They hold solving customer problems above all else and celebrate customer-oriented victories. At Cisco, technical innovation is clearly valued. The drive to solve customer problems fuels that innovation no matter where it leads the company, a mind-set that is reflected in the statement on all employee badges, "No Technology Religion." As one manager said, "Being able to listen carefully to create relevancy [for customers] is a more important business value than innovation." In line with this thinking, Cisco puts a relatively large number of employees in direct contact with customers, including groups such as human resources that typically don't interact with customers.

It helped that Cisco had the luxury of an existing culture of customer focus. Cofounder Sandy Lerner, in the company's earliest days, invented a customized multiprotocol router for a customer who initially found no Cisco products that met his needs. From then on, Lerner made it her mission to establish a culture where everybody, even those in units distant from customers, went beyond providing standard customer support to addressing specific problems. Consequently, even when the company reorganized its silos away from the customer in 2001, it was able to maintain enough interaction among units to ensure a customer-centric view.

At least half the battle of promoting cross-silo, customer-focused cooperation lies in the "softer" aspects of culture, including values and the way the company communicates them through images, symbols, and stories. Touting service accomplishments instead of, or at least in addition to, product accomplishments through company lore can begin to shift people's mind-sets. Cisco's employee badges broadcast a focus on customer needs, as does a well-known company legend about how Chambers was 30 minutes late to his first board meeting because he chose to take a call from an irate customer. Linguistic conventions may also be used to signify the value of the customer: Target and Disney refer to customers as "guests."

Another admittedly soft but powerful cultural tool for aligning employees around customer needs is to treat your workers the way you want them to treat customers. The hope is that people will adopt a collaborative orientation and customer focus because they want to, not just because they'll reap a financial reward. Cisco is highly egalitarian, reinforcing the notion that all employees are important, which makes them more likely to cooperate across silos. The company offers equal access to parking spaces, for instance, and designates window-facing cubicles for nonmanagement employees, locating supervisors' offices within the interior of the floor.

Of course, the softer cooperation-promoting measures won't take hold if the harder ones—power structures, metrics, and incentives—don't reinforce them. Power structures are notoriously difficult to change. For example, in a customer-centric environment, people who are close to the customer and adept at building bridges across silos should gain power and prominence;

but unit leaders responsible for products or geographies who had clout in the old organization won't hand over their customer relationships and concomitant power bases without a struggle.

That was the case at JLL. Before the company created the Corporate Solutions organization, power resided almost exclusively within the service-based business units. Even after the account manager position was instituted, final pricing authority rested with the units, which made it difficult to compete with multiservice packages. Although solutions ideally carry a premium price, JLL's initial intent was to better serve customers' needs by simplifying the management of real estate and to position the firm as a multiservice provider. However, when JLL created a package of real estate services, the price quickly mounted, resulting in sticker shock among potential customers, many of whom associated buying in bulk with discount pricing. JLL unit heads—who wanted to maximize their own return, not subsidize other units—refused to budge on prices. In some cases, package proposals were delayed, thanks to negotiations that stalled or ended in a stalemate that could be resolved only by those higher in the organization. In other cases, the packages weren't priced competitively, and the firm lost the business.

The issue of autonomy raised concerns as well. JLL's business units were accustomed to a high degree of independence. They protected their client relationships and had always been wary of introducing other services—even before the account management unit was in place—because delivery would be out of their control and they feared damaging the relationships. JLL took several steps to resolve those tensions. For one, it signaled the importance and value of the account manager role by assigning it to only very senior executives, including two who had achieved the title of international director, a distinction earned by less than 2% of employees. The firm also delivered a series of presentations at annual companywide meetings highlighting the significance of the role to the firm's growth.

To ease the pricing standoffs, JLL began in 2003 to allow account managers to provide input into the performance evaluations of business unit employees who touched their clients. At the same time, JLL took steps to retain some power and recognition for the business unit CEOs and, in the process, help them learn more about the services outside their silos and how they might gain personally from cross-unit sales. Unit CEOs, for example, were asked to oversee accounts on which their services were a particularly important component; in this role, unit heads were explicitly responsible for the performance of account managers. Because their bonuses were tied to the account managers' overall performance, the unit heads developed a clearer picture of the value contributed by services outside their silos. They were also required to meet regularly with customers to discuss their needs and the quality of the firm's service.

To support a shifting power landscape, firms must also embrace new metrics and incentives. The product-focused metrics most companies rely on—revenues, growth, and margins—don't reward cross-silo cooperation or customer centricity. Sales commissions in some organizations encourage managers to bring in new customers rather than nurture existing relationships, for example.

Cisco is relentless about measuring and rewarding employees on the basis of customer-related performance indicators. A Web-based survey helps determine the pre- and post-sale satisfaction of customers who buy directly from Cisco or indirectly through resellers. Survey questions focus on a customer's overall experience with and perceptions of Cisco, along with product-specific issues. Follow-up surveys with some customers explore their experiences with certain products more deeply. All bonuses are tied directly to these customer satisfaction data, so employees are encouraged to cooperate across internal boundaries. Moreover, all employees, including interns and part-timers, are eligible for stock options.

## Building Capability

Regardless of the incentives and cultural elements in place to enhance customer-focused silo busting, employees will fall back on their old competencies and ways of thinking if they haven't developed new skills. For example, even though one of the companies I studied told product salespeople to include new consulting-based offerings in their pitches to customers, the reps found it easier to give a superficial account of the new offerings or to omit them from their pitches altogether. Old habits die hard.

As a company becomes more adept at inducing coordination and cooperation across units, new skills become valued and desirable. Rather than highly specialized expertise, customer-focused solutions require employees to develop two kinds of skills: multidomain skills (the ability to work with multiple products and services, which requires a deep understanding of customers' needs) and boundary-spanning skills (the ability to forge connections across internal boundaries). Such generalist skills are typically not rewarded or developed in a product-oriented organization, so it's not easy to find customer-facing generalists. The companies that succeed invest significant time and resources in developing generalists. Furthermore, they map clear career paths for those who pursue this route.

At JLL, most of the first account managers had spent the majority of their careers in a single service unit within the firm and remained members of that unit even after becoming account managers. Consequently, they were not always deeply acquainted with the other businesses or able to manage service bundles skillfully. Account managers hired from the outside were generally chosen for their ability to execute real estate transactions, not for the breadth of their service knowledge.

To foster the development of boundary-spanning skills and cultivate a cadre of employees who could grow into the account manager role, JLL began to rotate individuals through the three remaining silos (before swapping the service silos for customer silos), forcing them to acquire greater knowledge of the products, services, and capabilities of each unit, as well as to expand their personal networks across the firm. For those already in account management roles, the company instituted training sessions through regular conference calls and meetings. Early sessions tackled relatively simple tasks, such as the establishment of a common vocabulary. Subsequent sessions focused on improving account managers' knowledge of each unit's offerings and on cross-silo sales skills and new metrics, including the first rudimentary client-based profit-and-loss statements. An unanticipated benefit of the training was that it brought the account managers together regularly, helping them to stop identifying only with their silos and to begin forming a group identity that enhanced their cross-silo networks. As a natural consequence, top management could see that account managers were assuming increased responsibility for a broader range of services.

Best Buy's shift to solutions selling entailed identifying and targeting five large, profitable customer segments: young, tech-savvy adults; busy and affluent professionals; family men; busy, suburban moms; and small-business customers. Each store was designed to suit the needs of its largest customer segment. A "busy mom" store, for instance, features personal shopping assistance and a kid-friendly layout. Stores targeting the tech-savvy offer higher-end consumer electronics and separate showrooms for high-definition home theater systems. When the company rolled out its customer-centric strategy, it conducted extensive training to help employees understand their store's particular customer segment. It also trained sales associates on basic financial metrics to highlight how their efforts on behalf of target customers affect store performance.

At the corporate level, Best Buy created a Customer Centricity University for senior officers who had not been involved with planning the new strategy. For those executives, Best Buy outlined the rationale for the new approach, including detailed financials, and held breakout sessions with the teams responsible for developing and executing the strategy for each customer segment. Over 11 months, all employees and contractors residing at headquarters, as well as many other corporate employees, participated in the program. It was then disbanded, its essential elements incorporated into the company's orientation program for new employees.

Enhancing skill sets is only part of the challenge of capability building. Companies must also develop attractive career paths that give emerging generalist stars a sense of identity and a clear route for advancement. Even specialists whose roles may not change much in the new organization will probably have to develop some generalist skills and learn how these could contribute to their advancement. JLL, for instance, at first had difficulty attracting candidates for account manager positions, largely because the firm had measured success and offered promotions on the basis of achievements within a unit. Job security was a major concern for potential account managers, as one of the first to hold the position explains: "One of the big fears was that these accounts don't last forever. So if a person left his or her specialized area of expertise to run an account and after three years . . . the firm was no longer providing services for that account, employees feared that that person would be out of a job."

JLL addressed the career path issue in part through its customer-focused reorganization—whereby the Clients group housed account managers in a well-defined unit with a clear career trajectory. Other firms have developed "talent marketplaces" to signal the value they place on generalist, cross-silo skills. Modeled after informal marketplaces used within law firms, academia, and R&D units, these forums match employees on a flexible basis with available positions or assignments, thereby allowing generalist and specialist career tracks to coexist.

## Connection with External Partners

The three factors we've discussed—coordination, cooperation, and capability building—are silo-busting tactics that align business units around a customer axis. But by redefining the boundaries of the company itself, firms can further fight commoditization in two ways: cutting costs by outsourcing all but core activities (and, in some cases, by finding creative ways to outsource them) and joining forces with companies that have complementary offerings to create even higher-value solutions, which command a larger price premium. Such approaches still require cross-boundary efforts, but the boundaries are between a company and its partners.

Starbucks continues to charge a premium for coffee, previously a commodity product, and exponentially increase the company's sales through intercompany relationships that keep costs low while expanding the firm's offerings. It chooses suppliers very carefully (quality and service take priority over cost) and then shares an unusual amount of financial information, using a two-way, open-book costing model that allows suppliers to see the company's margins and Starbucks to review the vendors' costs. In return, the company expects suppliers to treat it as a preferred customer in terms of pricing, profit percentage, and the resources committed to the partnership.

As for expanding its offerings, Starbucks seeks to enrich the customer experience through alliances with partners in a variety of industries. Its bottled Frappuccino beverage is manufactured, distributed, and marketed through a 50/50 joint venture with PepsiCo; its ice cream is made and distributed by Dreyer's; its supermarket coffees are marketed and distributed by Kraft, one of the company's main competitors in the at-home coffee consumption market. A more recent alliance with Jim Beam Brands brought Starbucks into a new drink category: spirits. In 2005, the two companies launched Starbucks Cream Liqueur, which is sold in liquor stores, restaurants, and bars, but not in coffeehouses.

Starbucks's boundary-expanding moves have extended to nonconsumable items as well. For several years, customers have been able to buy CDs at the stores, and the company recently began to promote movies as part of its ongoing efforts to become, according to the *New York Times,* a "purveyor of premium-blend culture." It sponsors discussion groups (with free coffee) and is considering selling DVDs, publishing new authors, and producing films. To coordinate these promotions and partnerships, Starbucks has formed an entertainment division with offices in Seattle and Los Angeles.

Finally, Starbucks has expanded internationally by leveraging not other companies' products and services but the capabilities of regional partners. Whereas the company owns most of its domestic retail stores, it allows foreign companies to own and operate Starbucks stores in markets where those players are already established. In 1995 Japanese specialty retailer Sazaby opened a Starbucks in Tokyo. In such cases, Starbucks provides operating expertise and control through licensing, while the foreign partners take on financial risk and advise Starbucks on real estate, regulations, suppliers, labor, and culture in the markets they know best. Sharing responsibilities in this way requires Starbucks to apply the principles of coordination, cooperation, and capability building to its external relationships.

Starbucks's relationship-building capability has enabled the company to grow far faster than it could have on its own. What's more, with just about every fast-food company selling premium coffee, and versatile and affordable new coffee-makers lining the shelves at Target, the company has been able to shore up its position by selling not just coffee but a coffeehouse experience, built largely around a series of partnerships and alliances that provide customers with an array of high-quality offerings.

Such relationships can be mutually reinforcing: As one company shrinks operations to cut costs—seeking partners to take on formerly in-house activities—its suppliers must expand their horizons by increasing the range of their offerings or finding their own partners to help them do this. IBM, even while taking over major back-office operations for large companies, has condensed its own core operations by outsourcing activities like repair and server manufacturing to contractors such as Solectron. Solectron, in turn, has expanded its boundaries by acquiring an IBM repair center in the Netherlands, allowing IBM to condense still further.

There are pitfalls to integrating closely with suppliers. Some companies—especially those that are unclear on their core values—give away too much. Others become captive to their key suppliers and lose the motivation to make ongoing investments in new technology. Some also find that they are funding the development expertise and scale that may allow a partner to become a competitor, as when cell phone supplier BenQ moved from making handsets for Motorola to marketing its own brand of handsets in foreign markets where Motorola already had a presence. Integrated partnerships can also be risky if companies put a lot of information into their vendors' hands, as Starbucks does. If trust on either side is eroded, one party could misuse the information.

In managing external relationships to avoid such pitfalls, it makes sense to apply the principles used to manage across internal silos—particularly the principles of coordination and cooperation. The challenges of internal and external execution are not exactly the same, but they share many themes, such as the need to find efficient ways of exchanging information and aligning incentives. So, for instance, Starbucks has a set of formal coordination structures to help information flow between partners. In addition to regular meetings between senior management on both sides, Starbucks has a dedicated training program for employees who will be involved in managing supplier relationships. To ensure that both parties follow clear rules for knowledge sharing, the company has created a handbook for suppliers, which describes the firm's purchasing philosophies and policies, along with the standards vendors must meet on eight criteria.

Cooperation issues may be even more central to external relationships than to internal ones, given the need to apportion value fairly among parties and the omnipresent risk of opportunistic behavior. Cultural fit lays the groundwork for cooperation, and efforts at cultural synchrony may begin even before the partnership does. Starbucks not only conducts a careful assessment of a supplier's brand and operations but also evaluates cultural fit, largely through an event called Discovery Day, when prospective partners come to Seattle to discuss cultural and other commonalities as well as differences between themselves and Starbucks.

In today's ever expanding and shifting business arena, and in light of a growing focus on customer needs, the definitions of what is inside a company and what is outside are no longer clear. But as our sense of firm boundaries evolves, so will our understanding of how best to breach internal and external barriers.

———————

There are few downsides to developing true solutions. The risk is that in the rush to stand out in the crowd, many companies forget that solving customer problems requires a deep knowledge of who their target customers are and what they need. Some customers are better off purchasing products and services piecemeal. Leaders at GE Healthcare originally targeted solutions at large national accounts—which, it turned out, bought largely on price. These clients almost by definition weren't good candidates for the solutions offering. The company consequently refined its target customer profile to focus on multihospital systems—with at least $500 million in annual revenue—that demonstrated a willingness to provide GE with meaningful access to the most-senior executives. Through this targeting, GE Healthcare narrowed its focus to just 150 of the roughly 400 multihospital systems in the U.S. health care market—giving primary attention to 50 accounts that included customers ready to enter into a contractual relationship with GE and those that exhibited many key characteristics and expressed a willingness to work with GE.

The lesson for GE, as for others, is that it doesn't pay to put the solutions cart before the horse of coordinated customer focus. To stand out in a commoditized market, companies must understand what customers truly value. The only way to do that is to break down the traditional, often entrenched, silos and unite resources to focus directly on customer needs.

**RANJAY GULATI** is the Michael Ludwig Nemmers Distinguished Professor of Strategy and Organizations at Northwestern University's Kellogg School of Management.

Originally published in May 2007. Reprint R0705F

# The Execution Trap

*by Roger L. Martin*

**THE IDEA THAT EXECUTION** is distinct from strategy has become firmly ensconced in management thinking over the past decade. So much so, in fact, that if you run a Google search for "A mediocre strategy well executed is better than a great strategy poorly executed," you will get more than 42,600 references. Where the idea comes from is not certain, but in 2002, in the aftermath of the dot-com bubble, Jamie Dimon, now CEO of JPMorgan Chase, opined, "I'd rather have a first-rate execution and second-rate strategy any time than a brilliant idea and mediocre management." In the same year, Larry Bossidy, former AlliedSignal CEO, coauthored the best-selling book *Execution: The Discipline of Getting Things Done,* in which the authors declared, "Strategies most often fail because they aren't well executed."

The trouble is, Dimon and Bossidy's doctrine—that execution is the key to a strategy's success—is as flawed as it is popular. That popularity discourages us from questioning the principle's validity. Let's suppose you had a theory that heavenly objects revolve around the Earth. Increasingly, you find that this theory doesn't predict the movement of the stars and planets very well. Is it more rational to respond by questioning the theory that the universe revolves around the Earth or to keep positing ever more complicated, convoluted, and improbable explanations for the discrepancy? Applying Dimon and Bossidy's doctrine rather than Occam's razor would have you going in a lot of unnecessary and useless circles.

Unfortunately, this is exactly what often happens when people are trying to understand why their strategy is failing, especially when consulting firms are involved. In fact, Dimon and Bossidy's approach can be a godsend for these firms because it allows them to blame their clients for any mistakes they might make. Firms can in effect say, "It won't be our strategy advice that will let you down but your implementation of that strategy. (To help you get around that problem, we suggest that we do some change management work for you as well.)"

Of course, lining the pockets of consulting firms does nothing to further most companies' performance. I suggest a superior way to proceed. Rather than doubling down on the prevailing theory to try to get it to work, consider the simple possibility that the theory is wrong.

So let's evaluate the idea of the brilliant strategy poorly executed. If a strategy produces poor results, how can we argue that it is brilliant? It certainly is an odd definition of brilliance. A strategy's purpose is to generate positive results, and the strategy in question doesn't do that, yet it was brilliant? In what other field

## Idea in Brief

The realization of a strategy depends on countless employees. So it's no surprise that when a strategy fails, the reason cited is usually poor execution. But this view of strategy and execution relies on a false metaphor in which senior management is a choosing brain while those in the rest of the company are choiceless arms and legs that merely carry out the brain's bidding. The approach does damage to the corporation because it alienates the people working for it. A better metaphor for strategy is a white-water river, in which choices cascade from its source in the mountains (the corporation) to its mouth (the rest of the organization). Executives at the top make the broader choices involving long-term investments while empowering employees toward the bottom to make more concrete, day-to-day decisions that directly influence customer service and satisfaction. For the cascade to flow properly, a choice maker upstream can set the context for those downstream by doing four things: explaining what the choice is and why it's been made, clearly identifying the next downstream choice, offering help with making choices as needed, and committing to revisit and adjust the choice based on feedback. When downstream choices are valued and feedback is encouraged, employees send information upward, improving the knowledge base of decision makers higher up and helping everyone in the organization make better choices.

do we proclaim something to be brilliant that has failed miserably in its only attempt? A "brilliant" Broadway play that closes after one week? A "brilliant" political campaign that results in the other candidate winning? If we think about it, we must accept that the only strategy that can legitimately be called brilliant is one whose results are exemplary. A strategy that fails to produce a great outcome is simply a failure.

As I hope to show in the following pages, the idea that we have to choose between a mediocre, well-executed strategy and a brilliant, poorly executed one is deeply flawed—a narrow, unhelpful concept replete with unintended negative consequences. But the good news is that if we change the way we think about the problem of strategy versus execution, we can change the outcome.

Let's begin by exploring the consequences of the prevailing view of strategy.

## A Misguided Metaphor

According to the accepted dogma, strategy is the purview of senior managers, who, often aided by outside consultants, formulate it and then hand off its execution to the rest of the organization. The pervasive metaphor that informs our understanding of this process is that of the human body. The brain (top management) thinks and chooses, and the body (the organization) does what the brain tells it to do. Successful action is made up of two distinct elements: formulation in the brain and execution through the body. At the formulation stage, the brain decides, "I will pick up this fork now." Then, at the implementation stage, the hand dutifully picks up the fork. The hand doesn't choose—it *does*. The flow is one-way, from the formulator brain to the implementer hand. That hand becomes a "choiceless doer."

A neuroscientist may quibble with this simplification of the brain and body (and of the true order of operations between them), but it's a fair description of the accepted model of organizational strategy: Strategy is choosing; execution is doing.

To make this more concrete, consider the example of a large retail bank. The CEO and his team formulate a customer strategy. They flow that strategy down to the bank's branches, where it is executed by the customer service representatives (CSRs) on a day-to-day basis. The CSRs are the choiceless doers. They follow a manual that tells them how to treat the customers, how to process transactions, which products to promote, and how to sell them. The hard work of making all those choices is left to the higher-ups. Those on the front lines don't have to choose at all—they just *do*.

Now consider an experience I had working with a large retail bank in the early 1980s. The bank was revising its strategy and, as a young consultant, I asked to shadow a teller to get a better sense of the bank's operations. I was assigned to Mary, who was the top teller in her branch. As I observed her over the course of a few weeks, I began to see a pattern in the way Mary dealt with her customers. With some, she was polite, efficient, and professional. With others, she would take a little longer, perhaps suggesting that they transfer some of the extra money in their checking account to a higher-yielding term deposit or explaining new services the bank had introduced. And with some customers she would ask about their children, their vacations, or their health but relate very little about banking and finances. The transactions still got done in these instances of informality but took far longer than the other customer interactions did. Mary seemed to treat each of her customers in one of these three distinct ways.

After a while, I took Mary aside and asked about her approach. "Customers come in three general flavors," she explained. "There are those who don't really like banking. They want to come in, do their deposits or transfers, and get out again painlessly. They want me to be friendly but to manage the transactions as quickly as possible. If I tried to give them financial advice, they would say 'That's not your job.'"

"Then there's the second kind of customer, who isn't interested in my being her friend but thinks of me as her personal financial service manager. This customer wants me to be watching her other accounts." She pulled out a drawer and pointed to a set of small file cards. "For those customers, I make up these little files that keep me posted on all of their accounts. This lets me offer them specific advice—because that's what they want from me. If I were to ask about their children or their hip surgery, they'd feel as if I were wasting their time or, worse yet, intruding into their lives."

"Finally, there's a group of people who view a branch visit as an important social event, and they've come in part to visit their favorite teller. If you watch the lineup, you'll see some people actually let others go ahead of them and wait for a specific teller to be available. With those folks, I have to do their banking, but I also need to talk to them about their lives. If I don't, it won't be the event that they want, and they'll be disappointed with our service."

Intrigued, I asked Mary to show me in the teller manual where it described this strategic segmentation scheme and the differential service models. Mary went white as a sheet, because of course none of this was in the manual. "It's just something I've tried," she explained. "I want customers to be happy, so I do whatever I can to make that happen."

"But for the middle segment," I pressed, "you have to make these files yourself, cobble something together that bank systems could be designed to provide." (Of course bank systems did eventually catch up, and banks created sophisticated computerized customer information files that looked a lot like Mary's file cards.) "And frankly," I continued, "other tellers and customers could benefit from your approach. Why don't you talk to your bank manager about the three segments and suggest doing things differently?"

That was too much for Mary. "Why would I ever do that?" she replied, suddenly impatient. "I'm just trying to do my job as best I can. They're not interested in what a teller has to say."

Mary had been set up as a choiceless doer. She had been given a manual that essentially said, "It's all about the transaction—just do the transaction and be friendly." But her own experience and insight told her otherwise. She chose to build and implement her own customer service model, understanding that the ultimate goal of the bank was to create happy customers. To do that, she had to reject her role as a choiceless doer. Rather than obey the teller manual and deliver subpar service, she decided to make choices within her own sphere. She had decided, dare I say, to be strategic.

But Mary understood just as clearly that she was in no position to influence the decisions made at the top of her organization. Although she had chosen to reject the conventional, her superiors had not. So the bank, which could have benefited from her strategic insights, was shut out. It's a pattern I have seen again and again throughout my career. Often, what senior management needed most—although it was rarely able to recognize it—was to have someone talk with the rank and file in order to understand what was really happening in the business. Senior management couldn't get that information itself because it had created a model in which its employees were convinced that no one was interested in what they had to say.

## The Choiceless-Doer Dilemma

The strategy-execution model fails at multiple levels of the organization, not just at the front line. Executives, too, are constrained—by the boards, shareholders, regulators, and countless others that dictate to them. Everyone from the top of the organization all the way down to the very bottom makes choices under constraints and uncertainty. Each time a frontline employee responds to a customer request, he is making a choice about how to represent the corporation— a choice directly related to the fundamental value proposition the company is offering.

So if we can't draw a line in the organization above which strategy happens and below which execution does, what is the use of the distinction between strategy and execution, between formulation and implementation? The answer is none at all. It is a pointless distinction that in no way helps the organization. In fact, it does great damage to the corporation.

## A Warning Unheeded

**MOST MANAGERS ARE SO USED** to believing that strategy and execution are distinct from one another that they are blind to whether the strategy-execution approach makes any sense. The notion that strategy and execution are connected isn't new. But apparently we didn't listen carefully enough to the great management theorist Kenneth Andrews, who established the distinction between the formulation of a strategy and its execution in his 1971 book, *The Concept of Corporate Strategy*. He wrote, "Corporate strategy has two equally important aspects, interrelated in life but separated to the extent practicable here in our study of the concept. The first of these is formulation; the second is implementation." Despite the warning that strategy formulation and implementation or execution are "interrelated in life" and "equally important," four decades later, the strategy-execution theory artificially conceptualizes them as separate. It is high time that we delved a little deeper into the twisted logic of our current approach. If we don't, we are almost certain to fail.

In some cases, employees internalize the choiceless-doer model and stick to it faithfully. The employee follows hard-and-fast rules, seeing only black and white because that is what she has been told to see. Her perception of what her superiors expect drives her behavior. She attempts to achieve faithful execution rather than basing her actions on choices about what would be best for the customer within the broad bounds of the strategy of the corporation. This constrains her choices, and turns her into a bureaucrat. Any customer who has ever heard the words, "I'm sorry, there is nothing I can do; it's company policy" or who has called an offshore service call center and listened to the faraway representative read through a script that's utterly unconnected to the problem in front of him knows the pain of dealing with a bureaucrat in a choiceless-doer framework.

In other cases, employees quickly learn the rules of the game and become mechanically obedient. Then they become disillusioned and disconnected. Meanwhile, managers, blinded by the rigidness of the strategy-execution model they have come to know, make high-level abstract choices and assume that everything else is simple implementation. They fail to recognize that the choices made at the top will beget a whole array of difficult choices down the line. If employees make sound choices and produce great results, senior management gets (and usually takes) credit for having put in place a great strategy. If, on the other hand, there are poor results (whether due to bad choices by management, by employees, or both), the conclusion will almost certainly be that there was flawed execution. The employees are players in a lose-lose game: little credit if their team wins, lots of blame if their team loses. This bind creates a sense of helplessness, rather than a sense of joint responsibility for success. Inevitably, employees decide simply to punch their time cards rather than reflect on how to make things work better for their corporation and its customers.

It's a vicious circle. Feeling disconnected, employees elect not even to try to share customer data with senior managers. Senior managers then must work around their own organization to get the data necessary to make decisions, typically by hiring outside consultants. Frontline employees find the resulting choices inexplicable and unconvincing, because the data comes from outside the organization. The employees feel even more disconnected from the company and more convinced, as Dilbert would say, that they are working for idiots. Senior management blames the frontline employees, frontline employees blame management, and eventually, everyone becomes belligerent. Management imposes executional rules and ways of operating that feel unilateral and arbitrary, and frontline workers act against the spirit of the strategy and withhold data that would aid in decision making.

In this cold, self-centered world, relationships between levels of the organization do not develop or develop with mistrust. Reflection tends to be limited to what impact those in the rest of the system will have on an individual's ability to succeed; the person does not consider his own possible contribution to the problem. Finally, leadership tends to take too much responsibility for success by planning ever more-complex strategies and ever more-stringent implementation plans, while the middle- and lower-level managers see these efforts, feel helpless, and back off from taking responsibility. These are some of the inevitable costs of the mainstream strategy-execution approach.

## Strategy as a Choice Cascade

To fix our problem with strategy failure, we need to stop thinking in terms of the brain-to-body metaphor. Instead, we should conceive of the corporation as a white-water river in which choices cascade from the top to the bottom. Each set of rapids is a point in the corporation where choices could be made, with each upstream choice affecting the choice immediately downstream. Those at the top of the company make the broader, more abstract choices involving larger, long-term investments, whereas the employees toward the bottom make more concrete, day-to-day decisions that directly influence customer service and satisfaction.

At the CEO level, the choice might be as broad as "In what businesses will we participate?" The CEO would consult and consider broadly—within the constraints imposed by his board, investors, company history, resources, and so on—and make a choice.

Let's say the CEO decides that the company will invest heavily in the U.S. retail banking business. Given that decision, the president of that business unit might then ask, "How will we seek to win in U.S. retail banking?" Her choice is still quite broad and abstract, but it is explicitly bound by the choice made above her. She decides that the company will win in the retail banking business through superior customer service. From there, yet more choices follow throughout the organization. The EVP of branch operations might ask, "What service capabilities must we develop to deliver consistently superior customer service?" If the answer includes ease of interaction for the customer at the branch, the branch manager might ask, "What does that mean for the hiring and training of CSRs and the scheduling of their shifts?" And the rep on a given desk has to ask, "What does all that mean for this customer, right here, right now?"

It can be a very long cascade from the top to the bottom in a large corporation. In the bank example, there would probably be both a regional and an area manager between the EVP and the branch manager. As the cascade grows, its structure and operating principles become more critical. For the decision-making process to work most effectively, each choice must be integrated seamlessly with the others. In this model, employees are encouraged to make thoughtful choices within the context of the decisions made above them. The approach rests on the belief that empowering employees to make choices in their sphere will produce better results, happier customers, and more-satisfied employees.

The choice-cascade model isn't nearly as pervasive as the strategy-execution model, but it is implicitly in use in some of most successful companies in the world. Consider Four Seasons Hotels and Resorts, one of the world's leading high-end hotel chains. Early on, chairman and CEO Isadore Sharp made the decision to build his hotel chain based not on obsequious service and formal decor but on a new definition of luxury. He decided, he said, "to redefine luxury as service, a support system to fill in for the one left at home and the office."

The problem, of course, was how to get employees at every level to make choices that realized this desired outcome. Traditionally, hotel employees were poorly paid and considered transient and replaceable. Most hotel chains treated their workers as choiceless doers who were told precisely what to do, when to do it, and how—while watching them like a hawk. But the choice-less-doer model would have been the death of Sharp's vision. He needed every employee, from chambermaid to valet to desk clerk to hotel manager, to make the choices necessary to create a comfortable, welcoming support system for guests. It would have been impossible to make a step-by-step instruction manual of how to create the support system he imagined. So Sharp set out a simple, easy-to-understand context within which his employees could make informed choices. The goal for everyone at Four Seasons would be "to deal with others—partners, customers, coworkers, everyone—as we would want them to deal with us."

The Golden Rule—which Sharp, like most of us, learned as child—proved to be a powerful tool for aligning the cascade of choices at Four Seasons within his chosen context. If a Four Seasons customer had a complaint, every single employee was empowered to make it right in the way that made the most sense to her and treat the guest with the concern and care she herself would like to receive. And Sharp has walked the talk, treating his employees as he would want to be treated, as he wanted his guests to be treated. He has done it, he says, "by paying as much attention to employee complaints as guest complaints, by upgrading employee facilities whenever we upgraded a hotel, by disallowing class distinctions in cafeterias and parking lots, by pushing responsibility down and encouraging self-discipline, by setting performance high and holding people accountable, and most of all adhering to our credo: generating trust."

In short, he did it by letting his people choose. The results have been remarkable. Four Seasons is one of just 13 companies in the world to appear on *Fortune*'s list of The 100 Best Companies to Work For every year since the list's inception. The company also ranks first in its category in the J.D. Power and Associates' annual Hotel Guest Satisfaction Index and is routinely honored in the *Condé Nast Traveler* Readers' Choice Awards.

Of course, this empowerment doesn't happen without some encouragement. Leaders like Sharp work hard to create a context in which people below them in the choice cascade understand the choices that have already been made and the rationale for them. Those at the top must also be prepared to engage in discussion—without dominating it—around the downstream choices at each level. This can be made more credible if the leader makes it clear to subordinates that the results from their downstream decisions affect not only themselves but also the upstream decisions on which their choices were predicated (see the sidebar "A Cascade of Better Choices").

## Creating a Virtuous Strategy Cycle

The choice-cascade model has a positive-reinforcement loop inherent within it. Because downstream choices are valued and feedback is encouraged, the framework enables employees to send information back upstream, improving the knowledge base of decision makers higher up and enabling everyone in the organization to make better choices. The employee is now not only the brain but also the arms and legs of the organizational body. He is both a chooser and a doer. Workers are made to feel empowered, and the whole organization wins.

This idea isn't new. Progressive management thinkers have been talking about worker empowerment for

# A Cascade of Better Choices

**UNLIKE WITH THE STRATEGY-EXECUTION APPROACH,** in which leaders dictate set strategies and expect subordinates to mechanically follow, the choice-cascade model has senior managers empower workers by allowing them to use their best judgment in the scenarios they encounter. But to effectively enable those individual choices, a choice maker "upstream" must set the context for those downstream. At each level, the choice maker can help his employees make better choices in four specific ways.

1. **Explain the choice that has been made and the rationale for it.** Too often we mistakenly assume that our reasoning is clear to others because it is clear to us. We must take the time to be explicit about the choice we have made and the reasons and assumptions behind that choice, while allowing the opportunity for those downstream to ask questions. Only when the people immediately downstream understand the choice and the rationale behind it will they feel empowered rather than artificially constrained.

2. **Explicitly identify the next downstream choice.** We must articulate what we see as the next choice, and engage in a downstream discussion to ensure that the process feels like a joint venture that is informed by a hierarchy. Those upstream must guide and inform those downstream, not leave them to make decisions blindly.

3. **Assist in making the downstream choice as needed.** Part of being a boss is helping subordinates make their choices when they need it. The extent of help required will vary from case to case, but a genuine offer should always be a part of the process.

4. **Commit to revisiting and modifying the choice based on downstream feedback.** We cannot ever know that a given choice is a sound one until the downstream choices are made and results roll in. Hence, the superior has to signal that his choice is truly open to reconsideration and review.

decades. But that fact raises an important question: With all that empowerment going on, why do so many people still think that execution is all that matters? One answer could be that the firms those people work for do a terrible job of empowering their employees. But if that were the only problem, they'd just need to empower more and everything would be fixed (in other words, use the same old theory, and just apply it more rigorously). This isn't really empowerment but rather those at the top trying to get workers to buy in to their ideas. As those in charge formulate their strategy, they work with change management consultants to determine how they can generate the buy-in they need. They produce workshops and PowerPoint presentations to persuade those below them to be enthusiastic about the chosen strategy and to execute it mechanically as choiceless doers.

Senior managers who focus solely on winning buy-in from those below them don't tend to ask themselves, "How would I like it if I were on the receiving end?" If they did, they'd probably realize that it seemed detestable. It violates the Four Seasons version of the Golden Rule. Employees don't like the buy-in approach because it creates an artificial distinction between strategy and execution. They are expected to sit there and act as if they enjoy being treated as choiceless doers when they know they have to be something else for this "brilliant" strategy and its attendant buy-in process to be successful. As always, upstream theories, and the decisions based on those theories, constrain downstream experiences. In this case, an upstream theory that divides a company into choosers and choiceless doers turns empowerment into a sham.

It's time to revisit and revise our upstream theory. The business world may be utterly convinced that better execution is the path to greatness, but in truth, a better metaphor would be much more helpful. Only then will the rank-and-file employees of organizations be free of the scourge of buy-in sessions. And only then will the promise of empowerment have a chance of being realized.

**ROGER L. MARTIN** is the dean of the Rotman School of Management at the University of Toronto and the author of *The Design of Business: Why Design Thinking Is the Next Competitive Advantage* (Harvard Business Review Press, 2009).

Originally published in July 2010. Reprint R1007D

# Harnessing Your Staff's Informal Networks

*by Richard McDermott and Douglas Archibald*

**IF YOUR SMARTEST EMPLOYEES** are getting together to solve problems and develop new ideas on their own, the best thing to do is to stay out of their way, right? Workers can easily share insights electronically, and they often don't want or appreciate executive oversight. Well, think again. Though in-house networks of experts—or "communities of practice"—were once entirely unofficial, today they are increasingly integrated into companies' formal management structures.

Independent, off-the-grid communities have proliferated in recent years, and many companies have counted on them to deliver creative solutions to challenges that bridge functional gaps. But in the past few years, outside forces—technological advances, globalization, increased demands on employees' time—have begun to undermine communities' success. Consider the rise and fall of an informal group of experts at a large water-engineering company located just outside London. Starting in the early 1990s, they began meeting weekly to discuss strategies for designing new water-treatment facilities. The gatherings were so lively and informative that they actually drew crowds of onlookers. (The company can't be named for reasons of confidentiality.)

The community initially thrived because it operated so informally. United by a common professional passion, participants would huddle around conference tables and compare data, trade insights, and argue over which designs would work best with local water systems. And the community achieved results: Participants found ways to significantly cut the time and cost involved in system design by increasing the pool of experience that they could draw upon, tapping insights from different disciplines, and recycling design ideas from other projects.

Too much attention from management, went the thinking, would crush the group's collaborative nature. But the very informality of this community eventually rendered it obsolete. What happened to it was typical: The members gained access to more sophisticated design tools and to vast amounts of data via the internet. Increased global connectivity drew more people into the community and into individual projects. Soon the engineers were spending more time at their desks, gathering and organizing data, sorting through multiple versions of designs, and managing remote contacts. The community started to feel less intimate, and its members, less obligated to their peers. Swamped, the engineers found

## Idea in Brief

If your smartest employees are getting together to solve problems and develop new ideas on their own, the best thing to do is to stay out of their way, right? Well, think again. For years, loosely organized employee networks have been helping companies find creative solutions to challenges that bridge functional gaps. Composed of on-staff experts who got together to share information and insights, these "communities of practice" often generated improvements that saved firms dramatic amounts of money and time. Not wanting to crush these groups' collaborative nature, managers let them operate independently, off the grid. But as business became more global and technology

multiplied the tools and information available to experts exponentially, community members found it harder to dedicate time to these voluntary groups. Communities started to fail. They didn't die, however; they evolved, becoming integrated into companies' formal structures. Today they're an actively managed part of the organization, with clear accountability and executive oversight. The most effective communities address issues that are critical to the organization and strive to meet specific, long-term goals. Companies assign them official management sponsors and full-time staff, train their leaders, and even make participation in them part of employees' performance criteria.

it difficult to justify time for voluntary meetings. Today the community in effect has dissolved—along with the hopes that it would continue generating high-impact ideas.

Our research has shown that many other communities failed for similar reasons. Nevertheless, communities of practice aren't dead. Many are thriving—you'll find them developing global processes, resolving troubled implementation, and guiding operational efforts. But they differ from their forebears in some important respects. Today they're an actively managed part of the organization, with specific goals, explicit accountability, and clear executive oversight. To get experts to dedicate time to them, companies have to make sure that communities contribute meaningfully to the organization and operate efficiently.

We've observed this shift in our consulting work and in our research. This research was conducted with the Knowledge and Innovation Network at Warwick Business School and funded by the Warwick Innovative Manufacturing Research Centre and by Schlumberger, an oil-field services company. To examine the health and impact of communities, we did a quantitative study of 52 communities in 10 industries, and a qualitative assessment of more than 140 communities in a dozen organizations, consisting of interviews with support staff, leaders, community members, and senior management.

The communities at construction and engineering giant Fluor illustrate the extent of the change. Global communities have replaced the company's distributed functional structure. While project teams remain the primary organizational unit, 44 discipline- and industry-focused communities, with 24,000 active members, support the teams. The communities provide all functional services—creating guidelines for work practices and procedures; publishing technical documents; and offering career development, access to expert advice, and help with technical questions. They are the first and best source for technical knowledge at Fluor.

Here's one example of how this works: Not long ago, a Fluor nuclear-cleanup project team had to install a soil barrier over a drainage field once used to dispose of radioactive wastewater. But environmental regulators mandated that Fluor first locate and seal a 30-year-old well, now covered over, to prevent contamination of the groundwater table. Poor historical data made it impossible to tell if the well really existed, and ground-penetrating radar also failed to discover it. Simply removing the contaminated soil to find the well would have been costly and risky for workers.

When the team posted a request to Fluor's knowledge communities, one of the experts suggested using an alternative technology from a different industry. The team tried it and found the well. In fact, within two months, Fluor went on to use the same method to locate—or prove the nonexistence of—more than 100 wells and suspected wells. Without the community's help, the project teams may have had to employ expensive, hazardous, and possibly ineffective methods. Any engineer can consult his colleagues, but Fluor's communities offer its engineers a worldwide network of expertise and connections no one person could build or maintain.

## Setting Up Communities Strategically

Unlike the independent and self-organizing bodies we saw years ago, today's communities require real structure. Though we once envisioned few rules, we have since identified four principles that govern the design and integration of effective communities.

### Focus on Issues Important to the Organization

Sustainable communities tackle real problems that have been defined by senior management. At pharmaceutical firm Pfizer, one such issue is drug safety. The company has about 200 active drug development projects, all in different stages, in different countries, focusing on different disease areas, and using different processes. To advise teams on safety, two types of communities work across these projects—councils and networks. About 20% of Pfizer's safety staff are involved in one or the other.

The nine safety councils focus on major organs of the body, such as the liver or the heart, or on key issues such as pediatric safety. On average, each has a dozen members, representing individual areas of expertise, with deep knowledge of toxicology, clinical development, chemistry, and disease categories. Councils are responsible for helping development project teams make difficult judgment calls on potential safety issues. Their members can be volunteers or appointed by management. They are, as Tim Anderson, Pfizer's head of Drug Safety R&D, told us, "the most elevated form of advice-giving body on safety." Membership in a council is a major recognition of expertise.

The dozen or so networks have voluntary, open membership and focus on disciplines or practices, such as lab functions or techniques; or on emerging technologies, such as nanotechnology. When the demand for advice rises high enough, a network can be elevated to council status.

Because they cross the entire development organization, safety councils and networks can take a "portfolio" approach to potential safety issues—comparing data, tests, and results on similar compounds being developed in different therapeutic areas. Sometimes they use tests and data from one team to support decisions by another, saving months of development time. The Kidney Safety Council, for instance, suggested that new biomarker tests could help assess whether a recent safety finding in an animal model had relevance for humans, which allowed one project to move to initial clinical trials much more quickly. Because the clock on patents starts at the beginning of development, shorter development time has a significant impact on product life span and business results.

In the nonprofit world, the United Nations has established a set of 12 communities that address serious social and economic problems in India. Solution Exchange is composed of people from governmental and development agencies and nongovernmental organizations (NGOs). Addressing issues like nutrition, education, and HIV/AIDS prevention, these practitioner communities now comprise 3,000 to 4,000 members each. They enable grassroots workers to share what they've learned about implementing programs with government agencies, policy makers, and other program implementers. The members' practical insights are increasingly influencing policy design and helping create more effective programs. "We reach more people through Solution

Exchange than any other program because it cuts across institutional barriers and allows people to connect regardless of source of funding, organization, or location," notes Maxine Olson, the former resident coordinator of the UN India team.

The communities also function like a research service, collecting and distilling timely suggestions for solutions to important problems. In one instance, members of the Food and Nutrition Security Community helped a midday meal program in the nation's schools by working with local growers to supply a steady stream of vegetables. In the rural south, one NGO created school kitchen gardens, where children were trained to grow vegetables on their own. The community spread these successful ideas to practitioners throughout the country. Since the typical Indian diet provides only 10% of the minimum required vitamins and minerals, the additional vegetables in school lunches led to real improvements in children's health.

### Establish Community Goals and Deliverables

Rather than inhibiting the exchange of ideas and information, formal goals and deliverables energize communities. They provide a focus—a reason to meet and participate. More important, they establish the contribution of communities to the organization.

At ConocoPhillips, communities report to functional teams, which are responsible for stewarding improvements in specific areas, such as oil and gas production. The functional teams, typically staffed by eight to 10 senior managers, have aggressive, measurable goals, like reducing the number of unrecovered barrels of oil. Each community owns part of the overall goal and tracks its progress toward achieving it. For example, when the company sought to improve the performance of its well operations globally, the functional team formed a well-optimization community, which then figured out how to reduce unplanned losses related to equipment impairment by 10% a year.

Explicit goals make communities operate more like teams on a day-to-day level, but community goals generally differ from team goals in that they're tied to long-term needs. Pfizer's safety councils assume organizationwide goals, which the project teams, with their focus on specific deliverables, could never meet. Pfizer's kidney council goals include developing a high-level, long-term strategy for research related to kidney toxicity; finding ways to share resources among kidney research projects; and evaluating external opportunities in kidney research, like strategic alliances.

**Provide Real Governance**

To be well integrated into the organization, communities, like teams, need strong, formal relationships with the organization's top leadership.

Companies often identify a senior manager to sponsor each community. This can turn out to be a dismal form of governance if those tapped for the role don't understand the purpose and value of the community and don't have the bandwidth to support its leaders. But if senior managers guide communities in a way that matches their long-term perspective, they can be very effective.

Pfizer's communities are sponsored by two senior managers, the heads of Drug Safety R&D and Safety and Risk Management, the two larger organizations the safety councils span. Both executives are highly engaged and meet semiannually with the community leaders to review goals, provide feedback, and understand the communities' impact and needs. For example, when one council proposed developing spreadsheets to mine 10 years of patient data that might reveal patterns of biomarker responses in clinical subpopulations, the sponsors suggested a more rigorous approach: creating an interactive relational database. The sponsors also ensured that the councils had the operational resources they needed, by providing them with two project managers who would help schedule meetings, track action items, maintain a website, and develop communications materials and training programs.

### Set High Management Expectations

However intangible, management's expectations have a strong influence on communities, just as they do on teams. Senior managers' sponsorship is useless if they're not genuinely engaged with the communities. In India, where each Solution Exchange community is sponsored by a local UN agency office, participation dropped when engaged agency heads were replaced by less engaged ones. Communities continued to thrive only when new agency heads were committed to them.

In Schlumberger, an oil-field services provider with 77,000 employees in 80 countries, each community has a management sponsor. Most sponsors are highly

## How Communities Differ from Teams

**COMMUNITIES OF PRACTICE ARE** different from teams, though less so than we originally thought. Like successful teams, successful communities have goals, deliverables, assigned leadership, accountability for results, and metrics. But they are distinct from teams in four ways:

1. **The long view.** Communities are responsible for the long-term development of a body of knowledge or discipline, even when they have annual goals. Teams, in contrast, focus on a specific deliverable.

2. **Peer collaboration and collective responsibility.** Community leaders establish the direction of the community, connect members, and facilitate discussions, but do not have authority over members.

3. **Intentional network expansion.** Professionals typically consult their peers for help with unusual or difficult technical problems. Communities deliberately seek to expand the internal and external resources and experts available to individuals.

4. **Knowledge management.** Teams typically do not have on-going responsibility for organizing and documenting what a company has learned in a domain; rather, they focus on a given problem. Communities steward the knowledge in their domain with a view toward solving problems that have not yet been discovered.

---

engaged with their community leaders and activities. The sponsor of a geosciences community, for instance, set six challenges for it based on the division's business goals. One was to publish a series of articles about Schlumberger's research in outside journals, focusing on topics that hadn't been adequately covered in the literature—a major undertaking for the community. At Fluor, management expects communities to be *the* technical resource for the organization and create its standards and procedures. In the words of John McQuary, vice president of knowledge management, "The community leader is the highest technical authority in the company."

## Maximizing Communities' Impact

Traditionally, organizations paid little attention to the operations of communities because they saw participation in them as a marginal activity, intended to benefit the members and not necessarily the company. But our research reveals that companies can increase the operational effectiveness of communities in four ways.

### Set Aside Real Time for Community Participation

Community leaders' biggest complaint is that they don't have enough time to execute their duties. When community leadership is a "spare time" activity, it can easily be squeezed out by more pressing priorities. Many companies have now made community leadership a formal component of job descriptions and performance appraisals. In our research we found that community leaders spend one half-day to one day a week on community management, or about 17% of their time on average. In a few organizations, community leadership is a full-time job. The UN's Solution Exchange communities each have a full-time facilitator and re-search associate.

Some companies link discretionary bonuses to community contributions; others make community leadership a necessary step toward promotion. At Schlumberger, part-time community leadership is one of employees' job objectives, reviewed quarterly with their managers.

### Train Community Leaders in Their Role
Leading a community is different from leading a team. Communities, our research shows, provide greater value when companies systematically train their leaders. In Schlumberger's communities, leaders are elected by the members annually. New leaders take a one-day course covering the aspects of communities that are different from teams—such as understanding how to find pockets of knowledge and expertise, how to engage volunteers in activities, how to grow membership, how to work with members external to the company, and how to influence operating groups when you don't have direct authority.

ConocoPhillips requires all new community leaders to attend a boot camp that outlines what management expects from them. The training starts by spelling out how community contributions connect to business goals. Then workshops review community governance, support, and expected deliverables and what the company considers critical success factors, such as establishing goals, engaging members, and setting results metrics.

## Hold Face-to-Face Events

A decade ago many organizations thought communities were a free way to develop knowledge. All the staff had to do was participate in an occasional meeting. But today most communities of practice include employees in remote locations. While they typically use collaborative software to link remote staff, the most effective communities also hold face-to-face meetings, which usually focus on specific goals. Face-to-face contact fosters the trust and rapport members need to ask for help, admit mistakes, and learn from one another.

Schlumberger enlivens its annual community meetings with competitions for the best examples of how the company's tools improved a customer's performance. Judges are drawn from the community's field, and the criteria for winning are clearly known: technical depth, business relevance, innovativeness of approach, and overall impression. Winners of local competitions participate in regional competitions, and the winners of the regionals compete in a global competition, for which they also write a paper. Last year 36 community representatives presented ideas at this small global event of about 100 people. The winning presenters received a monetary prize and an award from the CEO and chief technology officer.

## Use Simple IT Tools

Most communities don't need complex tools. Typically they use only a few functions, such as discussion forums, document libraries, expertise locators, on-demand teleconferencing, and online meeting spaces where members can edit documents as they discuss them. We found that simplicity, ease of use, and familiarity are far more important than functional sophistication.

---

When communities of practice first began to appear, we hailed them as a dirt-cheap way to distribute knowledge and share best practices. We thought they would be relatively self-organizing and self-sustaining, flying below the radar of organizational hierarchy. We thought they would flourish with little executive oversight— a notion that seemed to work well at the time. But as life and business have become more complex, we began to see that to make a difference over the long term, communities needed far more structure and oversight.

Despite this, communities remain more efficient and cheaper than other organizational resources and demand less oversight. In times when budgets have shrunk and managers are overwhelmed just dealing with the downturn, communities can be a valuable resource for coordinating work across organizational boundaries, whether across geography, as at Schlumberger and Fluor; across operating groups, as with Pfizer and ConocoPhillips; or down the value stream as at the UN in India. But communities are not as informal as was once thought, nor are they free. Though IT systems make global collaboration possible, successful communities need more. They need the human systems— focus, goals, and management attention—that integrate them into the organization. And they need to operate efficiently enough to respect experts' scarce time.

**RICHARD McDERMOTT** is the president of McDermott Consulting. He and **DOUGLAS ARCHIBALD** are associates of the Knowledge and Innovation Network at Warwick Business School in the UK.

Originally published in March 2010. Reprint R1003F

# Social Intelligence and the Biology of Leadership

*by Daniel Goleman and Richard Boyatzis*

**IN 1998, ONE OF US,** Daniel Goleman, published in these pages his first article on emotional intelligence and leadership. The response to "What Makes a Leader?" was enthusiastic. People throughout and beyond the business community started talking about the vital role that empathy and self-knowledge play in effective leadership. The concept of emotional intelligence continues to occupy a prominent space in the leadership literature and in everyday coaching practices. But in the past five years, research in the emerging field of social neuroscience—the study of what happens in the brain while people interact—is beginning to reveal subtle new truths about what makes a good leader.

The salient discovery is that certain things leaders do—specifically, exhibit empathy and become attuned to others' moods—literally affect both their own brain chemistry and that of their followers. Indeed, researchers have found that the leader-follower dynamic is not a case of two (or more) independent brains reacting consciously or unconsciously to each other. Rather, the individual minds become, in a sense, fused into a single system. We believe that great leaders are those whose behavior powerfully leverages the system of brain interconnectedness. We place them on the opposite end of the neural continuum from people with serious social disorders, such as autism or Asperger's syndrome, that are characterized by underdevelopment in the areas of the brain associated with social interactions. If we are correct, it follows that a potent way of becoming a better leader is to find authentic contexts in which to learn the kinds of social behavior that reinforce the brain's social circuitry. Leading effectively is, in other words, less about mastering situations—or even mastering social skill sets—than about developing a genuine interest in and talent for fostering positive feelings in the people whose cooperation and support you need.

The notion that effective leadership is about having powerful social circuits in the brain has prompted us to extend our concept of emotional intelligence, which we had grounded in theories of individual psychology. A more relationship-based construct for assessing leadership is *social intelligence,* which we define as a set of interpersonal competencies built on specific neural circuits (and related endocrine systems) that inspire others to be effective.

The idea that leaders need social skills is not new, of course. In 1920, Columbia University psychologist

## Idea in Brief

Your behavior can energize—or deflate—your entire organization through **mood contagion**. For example, if you laugh often and set an easygoing tone, you'll trigger similar behaviors among your team members. Shared behaviors unify a team, and bonded groups perform better than fragmented ones.

Mood contagion stems from neurobiology. Positive behaviors—such as exhibiting empathy—create a chemical connection between a leader's and his or her followers' brains. By managing those interconnections adroitly, leaders can deliver measurable business results. For example, after one executive at a *Fortune* 500 company worked with a coach and role model to improve her behavior, employee retention and emotional commitment in her unit soared. And the unit's annual sales jumped 6%.

How to foster the neurobiological changes that create positive behaviors and emotions in your employees? Goleman and Boyatzis advise sharpening your **social intelligence** skills.

Edward Thorndike pointed out that "the best mechanic in a factory may fail as a foreman for lack of social intelligence." More recently, our colleague Claudio Fernández-Aráoz found in an analysis of new C-level executives that those who had been hired for their self-discipline, drive, and intellect were sometimes later fired for lacking basic social skills. In other words, the people Fernández-Aráoz studied had smarts in spades, but their inability to get along socially on the job was professionally self-defeating.

What's new about our definition of social intelligence is its biological underpinning, which we will explore in the following pages. Drawing on the work of neuroscientists, our own research and consulting endeavors, and the findings of researchers affiliated with the

# Idea in Practice

### Identify Social Strengths and Weaknesses

Social intelligence skills include the following. Identify which ones you're good at—and which ones need improvement.

| Skill | Do you... |
|---|---|
| Empathy | Understand what motivates other people, even those from different backgrounds? Are you sensitive to their needs? |
| Attunement | Listen attentively and think about how others feel? Are you attuned to others' moods? |
| Organizational Awareness | Appreciate your group's or organization's culture and values? Understand social networks and know their unspoken norms? |
| Influence | Persuade others by engaging them in discussion, appealing to their interests, and getting support from key people? |
| Developing Others | Coach and mentor others with compassion? Do you personally invest time and energy in mentoring and provide feedback that people find helpful for their professional development? |
| Inspiration | Articulate a compelling vision, build group pride, foster a positive emotional tone, and lead by bringing out the best in people? |
| Teamwork | Encourage the participation of everyone on your team, support all members, and foster cooperation? |

Consortium for Research on Emotional Intelligence in Organizations, we will show you how to translate newly acquired knowledge about mirror neurons, spindle cells, and oscillators into practical, socially intelligent behaviors that can reinforce the neural links between you and your followers.

### Craft a Plan for Change

Now determine how you'll strengthen your social intelligence. Working with a coach—who can debrief you about what she observes—and learning directly from a role model are particularly powerful ways to make needed behavioral changes.

*Example:* Janice was hired as a marketing manager for her business expertise, strategic thinking powers, and ability to deal with obstacles to crucial goals. But within her first six months on the job, she was floundering. Other executives saw her as aggressive and opinionated—as well as careless about what she said and to whom.

Her boss called in a coach, who administered a 360-degree evaluation. Findings revealed that Janice didn't know how to establish rapport with people, notice their reactions to her, read social norms, or recognize others' emotional cues when she violated those norms. Through coaching, Janice learned to express her ideas with conviction (instead of with pit bull–like determination) and to disagree with others without damaging relationships.

By switching to a job where she reported to a socially intelligent mentor, Janice further strengthened her skills, including learning how to critique others' performance in productive ways. She was promoted to a position two levels up where, with additional coaching, she mastered reading cues from direct reports who were still signaling frustration with her. Her company's investment in her (along with her own commitment to change) paid big dividends—in the form of lower turnover and higher sales in Janice's multi-billion-dollar unit.

## Followers Mirror Their Leaders—Literally

Perhaps the most stunning recent discovery in behavioral neuroscience is the identification of *mirror neurons* in widely dispersed areas of the brain. Italian neuroscientists found them by accident while monitoring a particular cell in a monkey's brain that fired only when the monkey raised its arm. One day a lab assistant lifted an ice cream cone to his own mouth and triggered a reaction in the monkey's cell. It was the first evidence that the brain is peppered with neurons that mimic, or mirror, what another being does. This previously unknown class of brain cells operates as neural Wi-Fi, allowing us to navigate our social world. When we consciously or unconsciously detect someone else's emotions through their actions, our mirror neurons reproduce those emotions. Collectively, these neurons create an instant sense of shared experience.

Mirror neurons have particular importance in organizations, because leaders' emotions and actions prompt followers to mirror those feelings and deeds. The effects of activating neural circuitry in followers' brains can be very powerful. In a recent study, our colleague Marie Dasborough observed two groups: One received negative performance feedback accompanied by positive emotional signals—namely, nods and smiles; the other was given positive feedback that was delivered critically, with frowns and narrowed eyes. In subsequent interviews conducted to compare the emotional states of the two groups, the people who had received positive feedback accompanied by negative emotional signals reported feeling worse about their performance than did the participants who had received good-natured negative feedback. In effect, the delivery was more important than the message itself. And everybody knows that when people feel better, they perform better. So, if leaders hope to get the best out of their people, they should continue to be demanding but in ways that foster a positive mood in their teams. The old carrot-and-stick approach alone doesn't make neural sense; traditional incentive systems are simply not enough to get the best performance from followers.

Here's an example of what does work. It turns out that there's a subset of mirror neurons whose only job is to detect other people's smiles and laughter, prompting smiles and laughter in return. A boss who is self-controlled and humorless will rarely engage those neurons in his team members, but a boss who laughs and sets an easygoing tone puts those neurons to work, triggering spontaneous laughter and knitting his team together in the process. A bonded group is one that performs well, as our colleague Fabio Sala has shown in his research. He found that top-performing leaders elicited laughter from their subordinates three times as often, on average, as did midperforming leaders. Being in a good mood, other research finds, helps people take in information effectively and respond nimbly and creatively. In other words, laughter is serious business.

It certainly made a difference at one university-based hospital in Boston. Two doctors we'll call Dr. Burke and Dr. Humboldt were in contention for the post of CEO of the corporation that ran this hospital and others. Both of them headed up departments, were superb physicians, and had published many widely cited research articles in prestigious medical journals. But the two had very different personalities. Burke was intense, task focused, and impersonal. He was a relentless perfectionist with a combative tone that kept his staff continually on edge. Humboldt was no less demanding, but he was very approachable, even playful, in relating to staff, colleagues, and patients. Observers noted that people smiled and teased one another—and even spoke their minds—more in Humboldt's department than in Burke's. Prized talent often ended up leaving Burke's department; in contrast, outstanding folks gravitated to Humboldt's warmer working climate. Recognizing Humboldt's socially intelligent leadership style, the hospital corporation's board picked him as the new CEO.

## The "Finely Attuned" Leader

Great executives often talk about leading from the gut. Indeed, having good instincts is widely recognized as an advantage for a leader in any context, whether in reading the mood of one's organization or in conducting a delicate negotiation with the competition. Leadership scholars characterize this talent as an ability to recognize patterns, usually born of extensive experience. Their advice: Trust your gut, but get lots of input as you make decisions. That's sound practice, of course, but managers don't always have the time to consult dozens of people.

Findings in neuroscience suggest that this approach is probably too cautious. Intuition, too, is in the brain, produced in part by a class of neurons called *spindle cells* because of their shape. They have a body size about four times that of other brain cells, with an extra-long branch to make attaching to other cells easier and transmitting thoughts and feelings to them quicker. This ultrarapid connection of emotions, beliefs, and judgments creates what behavioral scientists call our social guidance system. Spindle cells trigger neural networks that come into play whenever we have to choose the best response among many—even for a task as routine as prioritizing a to-do list. These cells also help us gauge whether someone is trustworthy and right (or wrong) for a job. Within one-twentieth of a second, our spindle cells fire with information about how we feel about that person; such "thin-slice" judgments can be very accurate, as follow-up metrics reveal. Therefore, leaders should not fear to act on those judgments, provided that they are also attuned to others' moods.

Such attunement is literally physical. Followers of an effective leader experience rapport with her—or what we and our colleague Annie McKee call "resonance." Much of this feeling arises unconsciously, thanks to mirror neurons and spindle-cell circuitry. But another class of neurons is also involved: *Oscillators* coordinate people physically by regulating how and when their bodies move together. You can see oscillators in action when you watch people about to kiss; their movements look like a dance, one body responding to the other seamlessly. The same dynamic occurs when two cellists play together. Not only do they hit their notes in unison, but thanks to oscillators, the two musicians' right brain hemispheres are more closely coordinated than are the left and right sides of their individual brains.

# Do Women Have Stronger Social Circuits?

**PEOPLE OFTEN ASK WHETHER GENDER** differences factor into the social intelligence skills needed for outstanding leadership. The answer is yes and no. It's true that women tend, on average, to be better than men at immediately sensing other people's emotions, whereas men tend to have more social confidence, at least in work settings. However, gender differences in social intelligence that are dramatic in the general population are all but absent among the most successful leaders.

When the University of Toledo's Margaret Hopkins studied several hundred executives from a major bank, she found gender differences in social intelligence in the overall group but not between the most effective men and the most effective women. Ruth Malloy of the Hay Group uncovered a similar pattern in her study of CEOs of international companies. Gender, clearly, is not neural destiny.

## Firing Up Your Social Neurons

The firing of social neurons is evident all around us. We once analyzed a video of Herb Kelleher, a cofounder and former CEO of Southwest Airlines, strolling down the corridors of Love Field in Dallas, the airline's hub. We could practically see him activate the mirror neurons, oscillators, and other social circuitry in each person he encountered. He offered beaming smiles, shook hands with customers as he told them how much he appreciated their business, hugged employees as he thanked them for their good work. And he got back exactly what he gave. Typical was the flight attendant whose face lit up when she unexpectedly encountered her boss. "Oh, my honey!" she blurted, brimming with warmth, and gave him a big hug. She later explained, "Everyone just feels like family with him."

Unfortunately, it's not easy to turn yourself into a Herb Kelleher or a Dr. Humboldt if you're not one already. We know of no clear-cut methods to strengthen mirror neurons, spindle cells, and oscillators; they activate by the thousands per second during any encounter, and their precise firing patterns remain elusive. What's more, self-conscious attempts to display social intelligence can often backfire. When you make an intentional effort to coordinate movements with another person, it is not only oscillators that fire. In such situations the brain uses other, less adept circuitry to initiate and guide movements; as a result, the interaction feels forced.

The only way to develop your social circuitry effectively is to undertake the hard work of changing your behavior (see "Primal Leadership: The Hidden Driver of Great Performance," our December 2001 HBR article with Annie McKee). Companies interested in leadership development need to begin by assessing the willingness of individuals to enter a change program. Eager candidates should first develop a personal vision for change and then undergo a thorough diagnostic assessment, akin to a medical workup, to identify areas of social weakness and strength. Armed with the feedback, the aspiring leader can be trained in specific areas where developing better social skills will have the greatest payoff. The training can range from rehearsing better

ways of interacting and trying them out at every opportunity, to being shadowed by a coach and then de-
briefed about what he observes, to learning directly
from a role model. The options are many, but the road
to success is always tough.

## How to Become Socially Smarter

To see what social intelligence training involves, consider the case of a top executive we'll call Janice. She
had been hired as a marketing manager by a *Fortune*
500 company because of her business expertise, outstanding track record as a strategic thinker and planner,
reputation as a straight talker, and ability to anticipate
business issues that were crucial for meeting goals.
Within her first six months on the job, however, Janice
was floundering; other executives saw her as aggressive
and opinionated, lacking in political astuteness, and
careless about what she said and to whom, especially
higher-ups.

To save this promising leader, Janice's boss called in
Kathleen Cavallo, an organizational psychologist and
senior consultant with the Hay Group, who immediately put Janice through a 360-degree evaluation. Her
direct reports, peers, and managers gave Janice low rat-
ings on empathy, service orientation, adaptability, and
managing conflicts. Cavallo learned more by having
confidential conversations with the people who worked
most closely with Janice. Their complaints focused on
her failure to establish rapport with people or even notice their reactions. The bottom line: Janice was adept

neither at reading the social norms of a group nor at recognizing people's emotional cues when she violated those norms. Even more dangerous, Janice did not realize she was being too blunt in managing upward. When she had a strong difference of opinion with a manager, she did not sense when to back off. Her "let's get it all on the table and mix it up" approach was threatening her job; top management was getting fed up.

When Cavallo presented this performance feedback as a wake-up call to Janice, she was of course shaken to discover that her job might be in danger. What upset her more, though, was the realization that she was not having her desired impact on other people. Cavallo initiated coaching sessions in which Janice would describe notable successes and failures from her day. The more time Janice spent reviewing these incidents, the better she became at recognizing the difference between expressing an idea with conviction and acting like a pit bull. She began to anticipate how people might react to her in a meeting or during a negative performance review; she rehearsed more-astute ways to present her opinions; and she developed a personal vision for change. Such mental preparation activates the social circuitry of the brain, strengthening the neural connections you need to act effectively; that's why Olympic athletes put hundreds of hours into mental review of their moves.

At one point, Cavallo asked Janice to name a leader in her organization who had excellent social intelligence skills. Janice identified a veteran senior manager who was masterly both in the art of the critique and at expressing disagreement in meetings without damaging relationships. She asked him to help coach her, and she switched to a job where she could work with him— a post she held for two years. Janice was lucky to find a mentor who believed that part of a leader's job is to develop human capital. Many bosses would rather manage around a problem employee than help her get better. Janice's new boss took her on because he recognized her other strengths as invaluable, and his gut told him that Janice could improve with guidance.

Before meetings, Janice's mentor coached her on how to express her viewpoint about contentious issues and how to talk to higher-ups, and he modeled for her the art of performance feedback. By observing him day in and day out, Janice learned to affirm people even as she challenged their positions or critiqued their performance. Spending time with a living, breathing model of effective behavior provides the perfect stimulation for our mirror neurons, which allow us to directly experience, internalize, and ultimately emulate what we observe.

Janice's transformation was genuine and comprehensive. In a sense, she went in one person and came out another. If you think about it, that's an important lesson from neuroscience: Because our behavior creates and develops neural networks, we are not necessarily prisoners of our genes and our early childhood experiences. Leaders can change if, like Janice, they are ready to put in the effort. As she progressed in her training, the social behaviors she was learning became more like second nature to her. In scientific terms, Janice was strengthening her social circuits through practice. And as others responded to her, their brains connected with hers more profoundly and effectively, thereby reinforcing Janice's circuits in a virtuous circle. The upshot: Janice went from being on the verge of dismissal to getting promoted to a position two levels up.

A few years later, some members of Janice's staff left the company because they were not happy—so she asked Cavallo to come back. Cavallo discovered that although Janice had mastered the ability to communicate and connect with management and peers, she still sometimes missed cues from her direct reports when they tried to signal their frustration. With more help from Cavallo, Janice was able to turn the situation around by refocusing her attention on her staff's emotional needs and fine-tuning her communication style. Opinion surveys conducted with Janice's staff before and after Cavallo's second round of coaching documented dramatic increases in their emotional commitment and intention to stay in the organization. Janice and the staff also delivered a 6% increase in annual sales, and after another successful year she was made president of a multibillion-dollar unit. Companies can clearly benefit a lot from putting people through the kind of program Janice completed.

## Hard Metrics of Social Intelligence

Our research over the past decade has confirmed that there is a large performance gap between socially intelligent and socially unintelligent leaders. At a major national bank, for example, we found that levels of an

# Are You a Socially Intelligent Leader?

**TO MEASURE AN EXECUTIVE'S SOCIAL** intelligence and help him or her develop a plan for improving it, we have a specialist administer our behavioral assessment tool, the Emotional and Social Competency Inventory. It is a 360-degree evaluation instrument by which bosses, peers, direct reports, clients, and sometimes even family members assess a leader according to seven social intelligence qualities.

We came up with these seven by integrating our existing emotional intelligence framework with data assembled by our colleagues at the Hay Group, who used hard metrics to capture the behavior of top-performing leaders at hundreds of corporations over two decades. Listed here are each of the qualities, followed by some of the questions we use to assess them.

### Empathy

- **Do you understand** what motivates other people, even those from different backgrounds?
- **Are you sensitive** to others' needs?

### Attunement

- **Do you listen attentively** and think about how others feel?
- **Are you attuned** to others' moods?

executive's social intelligence competencies predicted yearly performance appraisals more powerfully than did the emotional intelligence competencies of self-awareness and self-management. (For a brief explanation of our assessment tool, which focuses on seven

### Organizational Awareness

- **Do you appreciate** the culture and values of the group or organization?
- **Do you understand social networks** and know their unspoken norms?

### Influence

- **Do you persuade others** by engaging them in discussion and appealing to their self-interests?
- **Do you get support** from key people?

### Developing Others

- **Do you coach** and mentor others with compassion and personally invest time and energy in mentoring?
- **Do you provide feedback** that people find helpful for their professional development?

### Inspiration

- **Do you articulate a compelling vision,** build group pride, and foster a positive emotional tone?
- **Do you lead** by bringing out the best in people?

### Teamwork

- **Do you solicit input** from everyone on the team?
- **Do you support** all team members and encourage cooperation?

dimensions, see the sidebar "Are You a Socially Intelligent Leader?")

Social intelligence turns out to be especially important in crisis situations. Consider the experience of workers at a large Canadian provincial health care system that had gone through drastic cutbacks and a reorganization. Internal surveys revealed that the frontline workers had become frustrated that they were no longer able to give their patients a high level of care. Notably, workers whose leaders scored low in social intelligence reported unmet patient-care needs at three times the rate—and emotional exhaustion at four times the rate—of their colleagues who had supportive leaders. At the same time, nurses with socially intelligent bosses reported good emotional health and an enhanced ability to care for their patients, even during the stress of layoffs (see the sidebar "The Chemistry of Stress"). These results should be compulsory reading for the boards of companies in crisis. Such boards typically favor expertise over social intelligence when selecting someone to guide the institution through tough times. A crisis manager needs both.

---

As we explore the discoveries of neuroscience, we are struck by how closely the best psychological theories of development map to the newly charted hardwiring of the brain. Back in the 1950s, for example, British pediatrician and psychoanalyst D.W. Winnicott was advocating for play as a way to accelerate children's learning. Similarly, British physician and psychoanalyst John Bowlby emphasized the importance of providing a secure base from which people can strive toward goals, take risks without unwarranted fear, and freely explore new possibilities. Hard-bitten executives may consider it absurdly indulgent and financially untenable to

## The Chemistry of Stress

**WHEN PEOPLE ARE UNDER STRESS,** surges in the stress hormones adrenaline and cortisol strongly affect their reasoning and cognition. At low levels, cortisol facilitates thinking and other mental functions, so well-timed pressure to perform and targeted critiques of subordinates certainly have their place. When a leader's demands become too great for a subordinate to handle, however, soaring cortisol levels and an added hard kick of adrenaline can paralyze the mind's critical abilities. Attention fixates on the threat from the boss rather than the work at hand; memory, planning, and creativity go out the window. People fall back on old habits, no matter how unsuitable those are for addressing new challenges.

Poorly delivered criticism and displays of anger by leaders are common triggers of hormonal surges. In fact, when laboratory scientists want to study the highest levels of stress hormones, they simulate a job interview in which an applicant receives intense face-to-face criticism—an analogue of a boss's tearing apart a subordinate's performance. Researchers likewise find that when someone who is very important to a person expresses contempt or disgust toward him, his stress circuitry triggers an explosion by stress hormones and a spike in heart rate of 30 to 40 beats per minute. Then, because of the interpersonal dynamic of mirror neurons and oscillators, the tension spreads to other people. Before you know it, the destructive emotions have infected an entire group and inhibited its performance.

Leaders are themselves not immune to the contagion of stress. All the more reason they should take the time to understand the biology of their emotions.

---

concern themselves with such theories in a world where bottom-line performance is the yardstick of success. But as new ways of scientifically measuring human development start to bear out these theories and link them directly with performance, the so-called soft side of business begins to look not so soft after all.

**DANIEL GOLEMAN** is a cochairman of the Consortium for Research on Emotional Intelligence in Organizations, based at Rutgers University. **RICHARD BOYATZIS** is the H.R. Horvitz Chair of Family Business at Case Western Reserve University. He is a coauthor of *Becoming a Resonant Leader* (Harvard Business Review Press, 2008).

**Originally published in September 2008. Reprint R0809E**

# Shattering the Myths About Enterprise 2.0

*by Andrew P. McAfee*

**DIGITAL COLLABORATION IS ALL** the rage in the world of business. Companies in every industry are adopting collaborative software platforms that enable employees to generate more and better output. A May 2009 Forrester Research study found that almost 50% of companies in the U.S. use some kind of social software, and a July 2009 Prescient Digital Media survey revealed that 47% of respondents were using wikis, 45% blogs, and 46% internal discussion forums.

Underpinning this trend is Web 2.0, a term coined in 2004 to describe the internet's capability to allow everyone, even non-techies, to connect with other people and contribute content. Facebook, Twitter, YouTube, and Wikipedia are the best-known examples of this trend, and they have become some of the Web's most popular resources. Three years ago, I coined the term Enterprise

2.0 to highlight the fact that smart companies are embracing Web 2.0 technologies, as well as the underlying approach to collaboration and creation of content.

Enterprise 2.0, which I sometimes call E2.0, refers to how an organization uses *emergent social software platforms,* or ESSPs, to pursue its goals (see the sidebar "What Is Enterprise 2.0?"). This definition emphasizes the most striking feature of the new technologies: They don't impose predetermined workflows, roles and responsibilities, or interdependencies among people, but instead allow them to emerge. This is a profound shift. Most companies use applications like ERP and CRM software, which create cross-functional business processes and specify—in detail and with little flexibility—exactly who does what and when, and who gets to make which decisions. E2.0, in contrast, requires companies to take the opposite approach: to let people create and refine content as equals and with no, or few, preconditions. Using ESSPs enables patterns and structures to take shape over time.

There are several benefits of ESSPs. The tools help people find information and guidance quickly—and reduce duplication of work. They open up innovation processes to more people, which is an advantage because, as open source software advocate Eric Raymond put it, "with enough eyeballs, all bugs are shallow." They harness collective intelligence and the wisdom of crowds to obtain accurate answers to tough questions. They let people build, maintain, and profit from large social networks. They allow executives to realize the dream of creating an up-to-the-minute repository of everything an

# Idea in Brief

Web 2.0 technologies are now a staple of social collaboration on the internet. In 2006 Andrew McAfee, of the MIT Center for Digital Business, coined the term Enterprise 2.0 to describe how organizations use emergent social software platforms, or ESSPs, to pursue their goals. However, some organizations don't achieve the many collaboration-related benefits that internal ESSPs can offer. After studying both successful and unsuccessful E2.0 initiatives, McAfee attributes most of the failures to five misconceptions. The first two myths crop up before an E2.0 initiative is launched. One is that the risks of ESSPs, most notably from inappropriate use, will greatly outweigh the rewards. McAfee makes the case that those dangers rarely manifest in practice. The other pre-launch myth is that the ROI of an E2.0 initiative should be calculated in monetary terms.

McAfee shows how Enterprise 2.0 can deliver valuable benefits in terms of developing human, organizational, and information capital—without a numerical ROI yield. The final three myths arise after an E2.0 project is deployed. One holds that people will flock to a collaboration platform once it is built. Success actually requires various types of top-down support, including active participation by senior leaders. Another is that E2.0's primary worth is in helping close colleagues work together better. In reality, the value extends to networks of expertise well beyond a user's inner circle. The importance of those far-reaching interpersonal connections also debunks the last myth: that E2.0 should be judged by the information it generates. Information is indeed useful, but E2.0's greatest advantage lies in transforming potential ties between people into actual ones.

organization knows. Underlying all these benefits is a style of interaction and collaboration that isn't defined by hierarchy and is relatively unconstrained by it.

However, E2.0 hasn't delivered results or even gotten off the ground everywhere. Many companies refuse to take the plunge because the possible drawbacks —the

# What Is Enterprise 2.0?

**ENTERPRISE 2.0 IS THE USE OF EMERGENT** social software platforms, or ESSPs, by an organization to pursue its goals. Here's a breakdown of what the term means:

- *Social software,* as a Wikipedia entry roughly characterizes it, enables people to rendezvous, connect, or collaborate through computer-mediated communication and to form on-line communities.

- *Platforms* are digital environments in which contributions and interactions are visible to everyone and remain until the user deletes them.

- *Emergent* means that the software is "freeform" and contains mechanisms that let the patterns and structure inherent in people's interactions become evident over time.

- *Freeform* software has many or all of the following characteristics: Its use is optional; it does not predefine workflows; it is indifferent to formal hierarchies; and it accepts many types of data.

---

misuse of blogs or the possibility of information theft, for instance—seem concrete and immediate, whereas the benefits appear nebulous and distant. In addition, many corporations have walked away from their E2.0 initiatives, for three reasons. One, doubts persist about the value of these collaboration tools even when they are being actively used. Two, ESSPs often seem unimpressive initially. Pages in corporate wikis read like documents in a binder; blog posts look like newsletters; and personal pages look like Facebook profiles. Three, many projects simply never took off. Employees didn't flock to use the new technologies, and sponsors wound up with digital wastelands instead of the rainforests they had expected. In fact, a 2008 McKinsey survey showed that only 21% of companies were entirely satisfied with their E2.0 initiatives and that 22% were entirely dissatisfied.

I have been studying E2.0 projects, both successful and unsuccessful, since companies started deploying these technologies in earnest four years ago. My research shows that, despite the failures, there have been striking successes—and that more big successes are possible if only companies would learn to use these tools well. Most initiatives fail because of five widely held beliefs: reasonable attitudes held by well-meaning people, not the handiwork of saboteurs. Nonetheless, data, research, and case studies show that the beliefs are wrong; they're the myths of Enterprise 2.0. In the following pages, I'll refute them, starting with two that crop up before an E2.0 initiative is launched and finishing with three that can take hold after deployment.

## Myth 1: E2.0's Risks Greatly Outweigh the Rewards

When CEOs first hear about how Enterprise 2.0 works, many become queasy about allowing people to contribute freely to the company's content platforms. They voice a consistent set of concerns: What if someone posts hate speech or pornography? Can't an employee use the forum to denigrate the company, air dirty laundry, or criticize its leadership and strategy? Don't these technologies make it easy for valuable information to seep out of the company and be sold to the highest bidder? If we use these tools, how can we avoid breaking agreements with partners about information sharing? What if rivals use customer-facing websites to air grievances or malign our products and service? Are we liable if people give incorrect information or bad advice on the forums we host? Won't employees use the collaboration software to plan social events instead of work-related activities?

Those risks all exist in theory—but rarely in practice. Over the last four years, I've asked every company I've worked with about the worst things that have happened on their ESSPs. My collection of horror stories is nearly empty. I have yet to come across a single episode that has made me wonder whether companies shouldn't invest in E2.0 technologies. One conversation I had was particularly telling. In late 2007, when I was teaching a group of senior HR executives, one of them said that leaders at her company, which employed many young people, became concerned about how employees represented it online. When her team poked around on Facebook, MySpace, and other sites, it found that employees almost always talked about the company in appropriate ways. The worst thing the team discovered was a photograph of a training session in which some account numbers were dimly visible on a blackboard. When alerted, the employee who posted it immediately apologized and took the photograph down. Even that wasn't necessary; it turned out that the numbers were dummies.

Four factors work together to make E2.0 horror stories so rare. One, although anonymity is the default on the internet, on company intranets attribution is the norm. Users are circumspect and unlikely to "flame" colleagues. If workers do misbehave, companies can identify, counsel, educate, and, if necessary, discipline them. Two, participants usually feel a sense of community and react quickly if they feel that someone is violating the norms. Counterproductive contributions usually meet with a flurry of responses that articulate why the content is out of bounds, reiterate the implicit rules, and offer correction. Three, in addition to an organization's formal leaders, community leaders form a counterbalance. They exert a great deal of influence and shape fellow employees' behavior online. Four, the internet has been in wide use for more than a decade, so most people know how to behave appropriately in online contexts.

If corporations don't believe that these factors provide sufficient protection, they can easily set up a moderation process whereby executives vet contributions before they appear. This precaution is common on customer-facing sites, where spammers and vandals can wreak havoc, but companies can use it internally too. Don't forget, e-mail and text messages are invisible to everyone except senders and receivers, but ESSPs make content visible and thereby turn the entire workforce into compliance monitors. It's a myth that E2.0 is risky; if anything, it lowers companies' risk profiles.

## Myth 2: The ROI of E2.0 Must Be Calculated in Monetary Terms

The one aspect of Enterprise 2.0 that I'm asked about more than the risks is the business case for it. E2.0 initiatives, like all IT projects, appear similar to other investment opportunities in that a company spends money to acquire assets (such as, in this case, servers and software CDs). But that's a surface-level matter; the company's deeper goal is to develop its intangible assets—notably its human, organizational, and information capital.

The value of intangible assets can't be measured independently, as several experts have noted; it stems from the assets' ability to help the organization implement its strategy. "Intangible assets, such as knowledge and technology, seldom have a direct impact on financial outcomes such as increased revenues, lowered costs, and higher profits," state HBS professor Robert Kaplan and David Norton unequivocally in their book *Strategy Maps*. Therefore, it's tough to create a business case for E2.0 projects by estimating the monetary return on investment. I have never met leaders of healthy E2.0 initiatives who wished that they had calculated an ROI figure, but I have spoken with many who described ROI exercises as a waste of time and energy.

Companies that are launching Enterprise 2.0 initiatives would do better to focus on three elements other than ROI:

- **Expected cost and timeline.** By now, managers know how to break down the cost of IT projects. They should also estimate how long the E2.0

effort will take, work out the implementation stages, and lay out the milestones.

- **Possible benefits.** The expected benefits from E2.0 must be stated, although descriptions needn't be as detailed as those for the features of a piece of software or as grandiose as the promised results from ERP and CRM implementations such as "organizational transformation" or "customer intimacy." (See the sidebar "Enterprise 2.0's Benefits.")

- **Expected footprint.** Managers should detail the geographic, divisional, and functional reach of the E2.0 projects they are planning.

These three parameters are usually sufficient to allow executives to make decisions about whether it's worth investing in E2.0 projects. Most have little trouble answering questions such as "Is it worth spending $50,000 over the next six months to build a broadcast search system for the company?" The answer won't be an ROI number, but managers can nonetheless address it adeptly. Walking away from the classic business case doesn't mean abandoning clear thinking or planning. However, it's time to replace the myth that E2.0 requires an ROI calculation with the fact that tangible assets can deliver intangible benefits.

## Myth 3: If We Build It, They Will Come

Given the popularity of Wikipedia, Facebook, and Twitter, many executives assume that their companies' collaboration platforms will also attract masses of people. They

# Enterprise 2.0's Benefits

HERE ARE SIX BENEFITS A COMPANY can get by deploying and using an emergent social software platform:

1. **Group editing** allows multiple people to collaborate on a centrally stored work product such as a document, spreadsheet, presentation, or website.

2. **Authoring** is the ability to generate content and to publish it online for a broad audience. Unlike sending e-mail, authoring is a public act.

3. **Broadcast search** refers to the posting of queries in a public forum in the hope of receiving an answer. People publicize not what they know, but what they don't know.

4. **Network formation and maintenance.** Social network applications keep people in touch with the activities of close and distant contacts. Whenever a user provides an update, it becomes available to the entire network.

5. **Collective intelligence** is the use of technologies, such as prediction markets, to generate answers and forecasts from a dispersed group.

6. **Self-organization** is the ability of users to build communities and information resources without explicit coordination by any central authority. This is the most remarkable benefit of Enterprise 2.0—and the easiest to overlook.

adopt a passive rollout strategy, introduce a few ESSPs, and formally notify people that the forums exist. They then wait for the benefits to accrue—and are shocked when nothing happens.

Popular as large Web 2.0 communities like Facebook are, they still attract only a tiny percentage of internet users. The main task that E2.0 champions face is to draw in a greater fraction of their target audience. That's difficult for two reasons. One, people are busy. Few knowledge workers feel they have the time to take on an additional responsibility, especially one with ill-defined goals and expectations. Two, employees don't know how top management will view their participation in ESSPs. Will senior executives value employees who contribute, or will they assume that those workers aren't interested in their "real" jobs? When the answer isn't clear, an unfortunate sequence of events unfolds. A few people start using the new tools out of curiosity or enthusiasm. They soon perceive that they're talking only to each other or, worse, to no one. Shouting into a void loses its appeal quickly, so they stop. The project is then considered a failure.

To avoid this outcome, I advocate the use of explicit recognition programs, incentives, and other types of top-down support for E2.0 projects. That's how the formal organization can show that it values employees' contributions. Leaders also should use ESSPs themselves. When senior executives allow their blog posts to receive comments and then respond to the feedback, or use social networking software to create a profile and connect with others in the organization, they're demonstrating their belief in E2.0. Similarly, when a company recognizes those who answer others' questions, it asserts that this type of work is valid and valuable. That E2.0 will automatically lure people is a myth; only when people know they're being heard by those who matter will E2.0 become mainstream.

## Myth 4: E2.0 Delivers Value Mainly by Helping Close Colleagues Work Better

Most companies currently use ESSPs to support people who are already collaborating. The Prescient Digital Media survey cited earlier, for example, found that E2.0's most popular uses are employee collaboration (77% of respondents) and knowledge management (71%). When those are the goals, a typical scenario is for the organization to establish group-editing environments for all the units—such as labs, workgroups, business units, client teams, and so on—that want them, or to let the entities set them up for themselves. In most cases, these environments are closed: Nobody outside the predefined group can see or edit the content.

However, this approach has shortcomings. Consider the types of interpersonal ties of a typical knowledge worker. She has a small group of close collaborators with whom she has strong professional relationships. There's also a large set of people to whom she has weak ties: coworkers she interacts with periodically, colleagues she knows through coworkers, and other professional acquaintances. Next is another, even larger set of employees who may be valuable to her if only she knew about them. They could keep her from reinventing the wheel on her next project, answer pressing questions, tell her about a good vendor or consultant, let her know that they're working on similar problems, and so on. Finally are the people who wouldn't become colleagues of the knowledge worker even if she had ties to them.

Picture a bull's-eye with four rings; it can represent these four kinds of ties. When an E2.0 initiative consists of closed editing environments, it ignores the benefits that the three outer rings can deliver. Network formation often happens in the second ring. Authoring and broadcast search convert potential ties into actual ones, so they extend to people in the third ring. And collective intelligence works across all four rings; even strangers can trade with one another in prediction markets and generate accurate forecasts. In short, the benefits of E2.0 technologies manifest themselves in all four rings. It's a myth that companies should focus on group editing among close colleagues; the reality is that Enterprise 2.0 is valuable at every level of interpersonal ties.

## Myth 5: E2.0 Should Be Judged by the Information It Generates

It's commonly believed that the value of E2.0 can be assessed by looking at the information it yields. Popular Web 2.0 resources reinforce this idea: Wikipedia is a huge collection of articles, Flickr of pictures, and del.icio.us of web bookmarks. All of them deliver value to users mainly because they're comprehensive and of reasonable quality. It seems logical, then, to judge an organization's collaborative software platforms with one eye on quality and the other on comprehensiveness. This isn't unfair, but it is incomplete. First, ESSPs often capture work in progress rather than polished deliverables. Wiki pages and blog posts will look rough because they're essentially drafts. They're meant to present raw ideas—not refined ones. People should be encouraged to air first-cut concepts in order to show what they're planning to work on, what they're interested in, and what they know. Second, content points to people. Imperfect or incomplete information is valuable when organizations can identify who posted it. The social connection is often the real benefit that E2.0 delivers.

In 2008, for example, Don Burke, one of the evangelists for the U.S. intelligence community's Intellipedia wiki, posted some questions on my behalf on his internal blog. The first was "What, if anything, do Enterprise 2.0 tools let you do that you simply couldn't do before? In other words, have these tools incrementally changed your ability to do your job, or have they more fundamentally changed what your job is and how you do it?" Most respondents stressed the value of the platform's ability to convert potential ties into actual ones. Here are comments from a few of them:

- **From a Defense Intelligence Agency analyst:** "These tools have immensely improved my ability to interact with people that I would never have met otherwise . . . People that would never have been visible before now have a voice."

- **From a National Security Agency analyst:** "Earlier, contacting other agencies was done cautiously and only through official channels. After nearly two years of Intellipedia, this has changed. Using it has become part of my work process, and I have made connections with a variety of analysts

# How Smart Companies
# Use Enterprise 2.0

**ENTERPRISE 2.0, WHEN IT WORKS,** delivers impressive results, as these four examples show:

- Office supply company VistaPrint started a wiki in order to capture what a new engineering hire needed to know. Because this knowledge base often changed quickly, the company suspected that a paper-based solution would become obsolete. Within 18 months, the wiki grew to over 11,000 pages and 600 categories, all generated by employees rather than by a knowledge-management staff.

- Serena Software encouraged its employees to create profiles on Facebook and other social networking sites, both to learn more about one another and to interact with outside parties such as customers and prospective employees. The company eventually attracted twice as many people to its annual user conference—and much better candidates for its job openings.

- The U.S. government has deployed ESSPs across its 16 intelligence agencies, which include the CIA, FBI, National Security Agency, and Defense Intelligence Agency. An internal report concluded that these tools, which include blogs and the Intellipedia wiki, are "already impacting the work practices of analysts. In addition, [they are] challenging deeply held norms about controlling the flow of information between individuals and across organizational boundaries."

- A U.S. gaming company set up an internal prediction market to forecast the sales of a new product. Consumer enthusiasm for new titles is notoriously hard to predict, but the market provided a good crystal ball. The 1,200 employees who traded in the market collectively generated a forecast that turned out to be 61% more accurate than the initial prediction, which had been yielded by conventional means.

outside the intelligence community. I don't know everything, but I do know who I can go to when I need to find out something."

- **From a National Security Agency engineer:** "There's now a place I can go to for answers as opposed to data. By using that data and all the links to people associated with that data, I can find people who are interested in helping me understand the subject matter . . . Their helpful attitude makes me want to help them (and others) in return."

- **From a Central Intelligence Agency analyst:** "The first aspect that comes to mind is the ease of sharing ideas and working collaboratively with intelligence professionals around the world . . . I am actively involved in an early-stage project that would be impossible without these tools."

These responses may not represent the views of the entire intelligence community, but they clearly illustrate that Enterprise 2.0 lets people find new colleagues by converting potential ties into actual ties. The new connections result from content posted on platforms but are invisible in the content itself. E2.0 doesn't only generate information; that's a myth. It also helps connect people.

———

Nelson Mandela wrote in his autobiography about a leadership lesson he learned from a tribal chief in South Africa: "A leader . . . is like a shepherd. He stays behind the flock, letting the most nimble go out ahead, whereupon the others follow, not realizing that all along they are being directed from behind." Similarly, E2.0 reveals the domains in which people are adept, allows some to show the way, and gets others to follow them when it's in the company's best interest. Enlightened business leaders will use these technologies to lead from behind; the rest will be held back by the fears that stem from believing in myths.

**ANDREW P. McAFEE** is a principal research scientist at MIT's Center for Digital Business and the author of *Enterprise 2.0: New Collaborative Tools for Your Organization's Toughest Challenges* (Harvard Business Review Press, 2009).

**Originally published in November 2009. Reprint W0911A**

# You don't want to miss these...

We've combed through hundreds of *Harvard Business Review* articles on key management topics and selected *the* most important ones to help you maximize your own and your organization's performance.

## 10 Must-Read Articles on:

**LEADERSHIP**
How can you transform yourself from a good manager into an extraordinary leader?

**STRATEGY**
Is your company spending an enormous amount of time and energy on strategy development, with little to show for its efforts?

**MANAGING YOURSELF**
The path to your own professional success starts with a critical look in the mirror.

**CHANGE**
70 percent of all change initiatives fail. Learn how to turn the odds in your company's favor.

**MANAGING PEOPLE**
What really motivates people? How do you deal with problem employees? How can you build a team that is greater than the sum of its parts?

**THE ESSENTIALS**
If you read nothing else, read these 10 articles from some of *Harvard Business Review*'s most influential authors.

**Harvard Business Review** Press

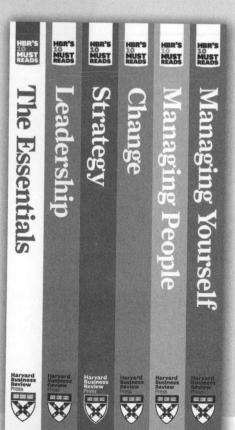